Sex,
Money
and
Power

OSHO FROM FULL CIRCLE

- Inner War and Peace
- Die O' Yogi Die
- Behind A Thousand Names
- Meditation: The Only Way
- Freedom from the Past
- Ah This!
- The Way of the Sufi
- The Silence of the Heart
- The True Name
- The Secret
- Truth Simply Is
- In Search of Celebration
- From Sex to Superconsciousness
- Never Born, Never Died
- Walk without feet, Fly without wings...
- Won't you Join the Dance?
- Priests & Politicians – The Mafia of the Soul
- My Diamond Days with Osho
- Tantra – The Supreme Understanding
- The Goose is Out
- Sex, Money and Power
- The Rebel
- A New Vision of Women's Liberation
- I Teach Religiousness Not Religion
- Words From A Man of No Words

Also in Hardcover

- The True Name (HC)

OSHO

Sex,
Money
and
Power

**FULL
CIRCLE**

SEX, MONEY AND POWER

Complies & Edited by Chaitanya Keerti
Coordination by Amano Manish
The sources of the talks reproduced in this volume are
listed on page no. 168

This New Edition, 2005
First Reprint, 2006
Second Reprint, 2007
Third Reprint, 2008
Fourth Reprint, 2011 *(New Format)*
Fifth Reprint, 2012

ISBN 13: 978-81-7621-163-5
ISBN 10: 81-7621-163-X

For Sale in India only

Published by **FULL CIRCLE** *PUBLISHING*
J-40, Jorbagh Lane, New Delhi-110003
Tel: +011-24620063, 24621011 • Fax: 24645795
E-mail: contact@fullcirclebooks.in *website:* www.fullcirclebooks.in

Designing & layout: *SCANSET*
J-40, Jorbagh Lane, New Delhi-110003

Printed at Yash Printographics, B-123, Sector-10, Noida-201301

PRINTED IN INDIA
05/12/06/07/10/SCANSET/DE/YP/YP/OP150/NP195

Contents

Introduction

"Religions contaminate your sex energy They start making you afraid that it is wrong, it is ugly, it is sin, it will drag you to hell. They want to dominate you; that is why they are against sex. I have no idea to dominate you. I am here to make you absolutely free."

Osho: The First Principle

Sex, money and power – these are the real basic issues. We face them daily. There is no escape from them, though we are always looking for escape routes. We seek the solutions in the scriptures. We listen to our priests, politicians and leaders who promise solutions but give us illusions, complicating the issues even more. Frankly speaking, they themselves are the root-cause of the problems. Following the advice of these priests and politicians makes us unnatural and we land ourselves in all kinds of perversions. This gives them authority over us. It makes us weak and gives them energy to dominate us. We become shackled, imprisoned into all kinds of taboos. Our whole society is nothing but an endless tragic story of restrictions, repressions and perversions. To enjoy life is wrong, to make money is wrong and ultimately to breathe and live is wrong.

And stories about these very priests are in the newspapers almost every day exposing their own perversions, their sex scandals involving the rape of minors, their abuse of the children under their care, their homosexual practices which the churches continually try to hush up but this news cannot be hidden forever.

Says Khushwant Singh, the author of many books and a senior journalist, in a recent article in his column "This Above All" in *The Tribune* and other newspapers:

"Flirting is non-serious. Sex is a serious matter. You may write about flirting but if you write about sex, you will be censured. Much worse, you will be condemned as a person with a dirty mind who wallows in filth. So a few, very few people dare to talk or write about sex because they know they are bound to be misconstrued and misunderstood. One man who had the courage to speak his mind on sex without caring what people said about him was Bhagwan Rajneesh known to his disciples as Osho.

"As a matter-of-fact what he says is very serious but has been trivialized by our *netas*, obsessed by wonky notions of social morality.... He is right in holding that our so-called civilized society refuses to accept nudity and sex as normal and natural. The more they are denied, the more they come to be indulged in secretly. We have become a Peeping Tom society. On the other hand, the so-called uncivilized, like our tribals, have natural and uninhibited sex and therefore do not create sex-related mental problems for themselves."

Khushwant Singh writes further: "Osho condemns this as a conspiracy of priests and politicians. Instead of priests who do little more than parrot platitudes about what is and what is not allowed, it would be fairer to cast the blame on religion as it is practiced." William Reich put it succinctly: "A happy life for the majority of mankind is impossible unless the power of religion is broken. Religion is the instrument used to impose an anti-sexual morality on the masses. It prohibits the most natural of pleasures and threatens those who break its commandments with dreadful punishment. One thing is certain: our sex life is poisoned at the source." Says Osho: "Sex should never be repressed. Sex should be lived in totality with joy, without any guilt." I say amen! He goes on to add, "...and suddenly it drops away."

Today, this country and the world may appear a little more free than how it was 30 or 40 years ago, when Osho shocked India with his talks in *From Sex to Superconsciousness*. This book alone created such an upheaval around the country and the ripple-effect reached to the farthest shores around the world. That brought a label of 'sex-guru' to Osho's name. The master who intended to liberate the world from the unhealthy and unnatural taboos received such widespread condemnation as his reward. The world may condemn Buddhas, the enlightened ones, but this does not stop them from being compassionate to the unenlightened ones. They keep on sharing their insights to the world, as they cannot do otherwise.

In this compilation, *Sex, Money and Power*, I have put together Osho's answer to the eternal questions, which are basically everybody's questions and problems. I am certain that the deep insights in this compilation will help the reader to grow more into consciousness, to understand these basic issues and live a rich and guilt-free life, with clarity and creativity, acceptance and joy.

Chaitanya Keerti

CHAPTER I

Sex:
The Most Vital Energy

There is a Zen story about two monks who were returning to their monastery. While walking ahead, the older monk came to a river. On the bank there was a beautiful young girl. She was afraid to cross alone. The old monk quickly looked away from her and crossed the river. When he was on the other side he looked back, and to his horror he saw the younger monk carrying the girl across the river on his shoulders. The two monks continued their journey side by side. When they were just outside the monastery gates the older monk said to the younger: "That was not good. That was against the rules. We monks are not supposed to touch women." The younger monk replied: "I left her on the bank of the river, are you still carrying her?"

Beloved Osho,

Would you talk to us about the alternative to suppressing or expressing our emotions?

Man is the only being who can suppress his energies – or who can transform them. No other being can do either. Suppression and transformation, they exist as two aspects of one phenomenon, which is that man can do something about himself.

The trees exist, the animals exist, the birds exist, but they cannot do anything about their existence – they are part of it. They cannot stand out of it. They cannot be the doers. They are so merged with their energy, they cannot separate themselves.

Man can do so. He can do something about himself. He can observe himself from a distance – he can look at his own energies as if they are separate from him. And then either he can suppress them, or he can transform them. Suppression means only trying to hide certain energies which are there – not allowing them to have their being, not allowing them to have their manifestation. Transformation means transforming, changing energies towards a new dimension.

For example, sex is there. There is something in sex which makes you feel embarrassed about it. This embarrassment is not only because society has taught it to you. All over the world many types of society exist, have existed, but no society, no human society, has taken sex easily. There is something in the very phenomenon of sex that makes you embarrassed, guilty, conscious. What is that? Even if nobody teaches you anything about sex, nobody moralizes to you about it, nobody creates any conceptions about it, still there is something in the very phenomenon that you are not at ease with. What is that?

First, sex shows your deepest dependence. It shows that somebody else is needed for your pleasure. Without somebody else that pleasure is not possible. So you depend, your independence is lost. This hurts the ego. So the more a person is an egoist, the more he will be against sex.

Your so-called saints are against sex – not because sex is bad, but because of their egos. They cannot conceive of themselves being dependent on somebody, begging for something from somebody. Sex hurts the ego most. Secondly, in the very phenomenon of sex the possibility of rejection is there – the other can reject you. It is not certain whether you will be accepted or rejected; the other can say no. And this is the deepest rejection possible, when you approach somebody for love and the other rejects you. This rejection creates fear. The ego says it is better not to try than to be rejected.

Dependence, rejection, the possibility of rejection... and still deeper. In sex, you become just like animals. That hurts the human ego very much, because then there is no difference between a dog making love and you making love. What is the difference? Suddenly you become like animals, and all the preachers, moralists, they go on saying to man: Don't be an animal! Don't be like animals! That is the greatest condemnation possible. In no other thing are you so animal-like as in sex, because in no other thing are you natural – in everything else you can be unnatural. You are eating food. We have created so much sophistication about eating that you are not like animals. The basic thing is like the animal; but your tables, your table manners, the whole culture, the etiquette you have created around food is just to make it distinct from animals. Animals like to eat alone. So, every society creates in the mind of every individual that to eat alone is not good. Share, eat with the family, eat with friends, invite guests. No animal is interested in guests, in friends, in family. Whenever an animal is eating he wants nobody to come near; he goes into loneliness.

If a man wants to eat alone you will say he is animal-like, he doesn't want to share. His habit of eating is natural, not sophisticated. Around food we have created so much sophistication that hunger has become less important, taste has become more important. No animal bothers about the taste. Hunger is a basic necessity – hunger is fulfilled, the animal is satisfied. But not man – as if hunger is not the point; something else is the point. More important is taste, more important are manners, more important how you eat, not what you eat.

In everything else man has created his own artificial world around him. Animals are naked – that's why we don't want to be nude. And if somebody is nude, suddenly he hits our civilization totally, he cuts the very roots. That's why there is so much antagonism against naked people – all over the world.

If you go and move naked in the street, you are not hurting anybody, you are not doing any violence to anybody; you are absolutely innocent. But immediately the police will come, the whole surrounding will become agitated. You will be caught and beaten and put into jail. But you have not done anything at all! A crime happens when you DO something. You have not been doing anything, simply walking naked! But why does society get so angry? The society is not so angry even against a murderer. This is strange. But a naked man... and society is absolutely angry.

It is because murder is still human. No animal murders. They kill for eating, but they don't murder. And no animal murders his own species, only man. So it is human, the society can accept it. But nudity the society cannot accept, because suddenly the naked man makes you aware that you are all animals. Howsoever hidden behind clothes, the animal is there, the nude, the naked animal is there, the naked ape is there.

You are against the nude man not because he is nude but because he makes you aware of your nudity – and the ego is hurt. Clothed, man is not an animal. With eating habits and manners, man is not an animal. With language, morality, philosophy and religion, man is not an animal.

The most religious thing is to go to a church, to a temple, to pray. Why is it so religious? Because no animal goes to a church and no animal prays; it is absolutely human. Going to a temple to pray, this makes the distinction absolute, that you are not animals.

But sex is animal activity. Whatsoever you do, howsoever you hide it, whatsoever you create around it, the basic fact remains animal. And when you move into it, you become like animals. Because of this fact many people cannot enjoy sex. They cannot become totally animal. Their ego won't allow it. So ego and sex, this is the conflict – sex versus ego. The more egoistic a person is, the more he is against sex. The less egoistic a person is, the more involved he is in sex. But even the lesser egoist feels a guilt – feels less, but still feels something is wrong.

When one moves deeply into sex the ego is lost, and as the moment comes nearer when the ego is disappearing, fear grips you.

So people make love, go into sex, not deeply, not really. They just make a superficial show that they are making love, because if you REALLY make love, all civilization will have to be dropped. Your mind will have to be put aside – your religion, philosophy, everything. Suddenly, you will feel a wild animal is born within you. A roar will come to you. You may start actually roaring like a wild animal – screaming, groaning. And if you allow it, language will disappear. Sounds will be there, just like birds or animals making sounds. Suddenly, the whole civilization of a million years is dropped. You are again standing like an animal, in a wild world. There is fear. And because of that fear love has become almost impossible. And the fear is real – because when you lose the ego you are almost insane; you become wild, and then anything can happen. And you KNOW that anything can happen. You may even kill, murder your beloved, you may start eating her body, because then controls are removed.

Suppression seems to be the easiest way to avoid all this. Suppress, or allow only as much as will not lead you into danger – just a part of it which can be controlled always. And you remain in control, you manipulate. You allow up to an extent and then you don't allow. Then you close yourself and shut yourself.

Suppression exists as a protection, as a safeguard, as a security measure, and religions have used this security measure. They have exploited this fear of sex and they have made you more afraid. They have created an inner trembling. They have made sex the basic sin and they say: Unless sex disappears, you will not be able to enter into the Kingdom of God. They are true, in a sense, and still wrong.

I also say unless sex disappears you will not be able to enter into the Kingdom of God. But sex disappears only when you have accepted it totally – not suppressed, but transformed it.

Religions have exploited human fear and the human tendency to be egoistic. They have created many techniques to suppress. It is not very difficult to suppress, but it is very costly – because your whole energy becomes divided against itself, fighting, and then the whole life is dissipated.

Sex is the most vital energy, the only energy I say, which you have. Don't fight with it – it will be a waste of life and time – rather transform it. But how to do it? How to transform it? What can we do? If you have understood the fear, then you can understand the clue, what can be done. The fear is there because you feel that the control will be lost, and once the control is lost you cannot do anything. I teach you a new control: the control of the witnessing self, not the control of a manipulating mind, but the control of a witnessing self. And I tell you that control is the supreme possible and that control is so natural that you never feel you are controlling. The control happens spontaneously with witnessing. Move into sex but be a witness. The only thing to remember is: I must encounter the whole process, I must see through it, I must remain a witness, I should not become unconscious – that's all. Become wild, but don't become unconscious. Then there is no danger in wildness; then wildness is beautiful. Really, only a wild man can be beautiful. A woman who is not wild cannot be beautiful – because the more wild, the more alive. Then you are just like a wild tiger, or a wild deer running in the forest... and the beauty of it!

But the problem is: not to become unconscious. If you become unconscious, then you are under unconscious forces, then you are under the forces of karma. Whatsoever you have done in the past is accumulated there. That accumulated conditioning can take grip of you and move you in certain directions which will be dangerous for you and for others. But if you remain a witness, that past conditioning cannot interfere.

So the whole method, or the whole process of becoming a witness, is the process of transforming the sex energy. Moving into sex, remain alert. Whatsoever is happening, observe it, see through it; don't miss a single point. Whatsoever is happening in your body, in your mind, in your inner energy the new circuit is being made, the body electricity is moving in a new way, in a new circular way; now the body electricity has become one with the partner, with the wife, with the consort. And now an inner circle is created – and you can feel it. If you are alert, you can feel it. You will feel that you have become a vehicle of a vital energy moving. Remain alert. Soon you will become aware that the more the circuit is created, the more thoughts are dropping; they are dropping like yellow leaves from a tree. Thoughts are dropping. The mind is becoming more and more empty.

Remain alert and soon you will see that you are but there is no ego. You cannot say I. Something greater than you has happened to you. You and your partner, both have dissolved into that greater energy.

But this merger should not become unconscious, otherwise you miss the point. Then it is a beautiful sex act, but no transformation. It is beautiful, nothing is wrong in it, but it is not transformation. And if it is unconscious then you will always be moving in a rut. Again and again you will want to have this experience. The experience is beautiful as far as it goes, but it will become a routine. And each time you have it, again more desire is created. The more you have it, the more you desire it, and you move in a vicious circle. You don't grow, you just rotate.

Rotation is bad, because then growth is not happening. Then energy is simply wasted. Even if the experience is good the energy is wasted, because much more was possible. And it was just at the corner, just a turn, and much more was possible. With the same energy the divine could have been achieved. With the same energy the ultimate ecstasy is possible, and you are wasting that energy in momentary experiences. And by and by, those experiences will become boring; because repeated again and again, everything becomes boring. When the newness is lost, boredom is created. If you remain alert you will see: first, changes of energy in the body; second, dropping of thoughts from the mind; and third, dropping of the ego from the heart.

These three things have to be observed, watched carefully. And when the third has happened sex energy has become meditative energy. Now you are no longer in sex. You may be lying with your beloved, bodies together, but you are no more there – you are transplanted into a new world. This is what Shiva goes on talking about in VIGYAN BHAIRAVTANTRA and in other tantra books. He goes on talking about this phenomenon: you are transmuted, a mutation has happened. This will happen through witnessing. If you follow suppression, you can become so-called human beings – bogus, superficial, hollow within; just dummies, not authentic, not real. If you don't follow suppression but follow indulgence, you will become like an animal – beautiful, more beautiful than so-called civilized man, but just animals – not alert, not aware, not conscious of the possibility of growth, of the human potential.

If you transform the energy, then you become divine. And remember, when I say divine, both things are implied in it. The wild animal with its total beauty of being is there. That wild animal is not rejected and denied. He is there – richer, because he is more alert. So all the wildness is there and the beauty of it. And all that civilization has been trying to force is there, but spontaneous, not forced. Once the energy is transformed, nature and God meet in you – nature with its beauty, God with total grace. This is what a sage means. A sage means a meeting of nature and the divine, a meeting of the created and the creator, a meeting of body and soul, a meeting of that which is below and of that which is above, a meeting of the earth and the sky.

Says Lao Tzu: Tao happens when earth and heaven meet. This is the meeting. Witnessing is the basic source. But it will be difficult to become a witness in the sex act if you are not trying to become a witness in other acts of your life. So try it the whole day, otherwise you will be in self-deception. If you cannot become a witness while walking on the road, don't try to deceive yourself you cannot become a witness while making love. If just walking on the road, such a simple process, and you cannot become a witness – you become unconscious in it – how can you become a witness while making love? The process is so deep... you will fall unconscious. You fall unconscious while walking on the road. Try it: even for a few seconds you will not be able to remember. Try it; walking on the road just try: I will remember I am walking, I am walking, I am walking. After a few seconds you have forgotten. Something else has popped into the mind, you have followed some other direction, you have completely forgotten. And suddenly you remember: I have forgotten. So if such a small act like walking cannot be made conscious, it is going to be difficult to make love a conscious meditation.

So try with simple things, simple activities. While eating, try it. While walking, try it. While talking, listening, try it. Try from everywhere. Make it a constant hammering inside; let your whole body and mind know that you are making an effort to be alert.

Only then some day in love the witness will happen. And when it happens, ecstasy has happened to you — the first glimpse of the divine has descended upon you. From that moment onwards sex will not be sex at all. And sooner or later sex will disappear. This disappearance gives you BRAHMACHARYA – then you become a celibate.

Monks in the Catholic monasteries, or monks following traditional Jainism, or other types of monks, are only celibates for name's sake, because their mind goes on making love – more so than your mind. For them, sex becomes cerebral, which is the worst possible thing that can happen, because it is a perversion. If you THINK about sex, it is a perversion. Making love is natural; thinking about it, constantly being involved with sex inside the mind, is a perversion. The so-called monks are perverted beings, not because they are monks, but because they have chosen the path of suppression, which is a wrong path, which leads nowhere. Jesus, Mahavira, or Buddha, they are following the path of witnessing. Then brahmacharya happens. This word "brahmacharya" is very beautiful. The very word means: the way the divine behaves. The way the divine behaves – brahmacharya. It has nothing to say against sex; the word is not against sex at all. The word simply says this is how the divine acts, behaves, moves, walks.

Once you have known the *satori* that is possible by witnessing the sex act, your whole life will be transformed, you will start behaving like a god. What are the characteristics of the behavior of a god? How does the divine behave?

One thing: he is not dependent, he is absolutely independent. He gives his love to you, but this is not a need. He gives out of his abundance, he has too much. You simply unburden him if you take it, but this is not a need. And the god is a creator. Whenever sex has become a transformed force, your life becomes creative. Sex is creative force. Right now it moves into biology; it creates new beings, it gives birth. When there is no sex and the energy is transforming, it moves into a new world of creativity. Then many new dimensions of creativity become open to you. It is not that you will start painting, or making poetry, or doing something else – not that. It may happen, it may not happen, but whatsoever you do will become a creative act, whatsoever you do will become artistic. Even Buddha sitting under his bodhi tree, not doing anything, is creative. The WAY he is sitting, the very way he is sitting there, he is creating a force, an energy, vibrations all around him.

Much research has been done recently on Egyptian pyramids, and they have come to know many mysterious facts. One of the facts is that the shape of the pyramid, the very shape, is mysterious. Suddenly, scientists became aware that if you put a dead body in a pyramid it will be preserved without any chemicals; just the shape helps preservation.

Then one scientist in Germany thought: If the shape can do so much that the body is preserved automatically – just by the shape, just the pressure of the shape.... So he tried it on his razor blade. He made a small pyramid, a cardboard pyramid, and tried it with his used razor blade. Within hours the razor blade was again ready to be used. The shape, had given sharpness again to the blade. Then he patented it.

One razor blade can be used for your whole life: you just put it in the pyramid. Nothing is to be done; just the shape gives sharpness again, again and again. Now scientists say that every shape creates a particular milieu. A Buddha is sitting under a bodhi tree: the way he sits, the posture, the gesture, the very phenomenon of his being there without any ego, is creating millions of vibrations around. They will go on spreading. Even when this Buddha has disappeared from this tree, those vibrations will go on and on and on – they will touch other planets and other stars. Wherever a Buddha vibration touches it is creative, it gives you a thrill, it gives you a new breeze.

When sex energy is transformed, your whole life becomes creative – independent, free, creative. Whatsoever you do, you create through it. Even if you do not do anything, non-doing becomes creative. Just your very being creates much that is beautiful, that is true, that is good.

Now the story. The old monk who says to the younger: This is against the rules, you should not have touched the girl, is not only saying so because of the rules. Many things are implied. He is rationalizing; he is feeling jealous. And this is how the human mind works – you cannot say directly that you are feeling jealous.

The girl, a beautiful girl, was standing near the river. The sun was setting, down and down, and the girl was afraid. Then came this old monk who was going to his monastery. He looked at the girl, because it is very difficult for a monk to miss a girl and not to look at her. Very difficult for a monk, he is so obsessed with women! He is fighting hard; he is constantly aware that the enemy is there in the woman.

You can miss a friend but you cannot miss an enemy – you have to see him. If you pass down the street and the enemy is there, it is impossible not to see him. Friends can be passed without even becoming aware that they are there. But enemies, no – because with the enemy is fear. And a beautiful girl, standing lonely, nobody else! The girl wanted somebody to help her – the river was unknown and she was afraid to cross it.

This old man must have tried to close his eyes,

SEX, MONEY AND POWER

must have tried to close his heart, must have tried to close his sex centre, because that is the only protection against the enemy. He must have hurried, he must have avoided looking back. But when you avoid, you look; when you try NOT to look, you are looking.

His whole mind was filled with the girl. His whole being was around the girl. He was passing the river, but he was not aware of the river now – he could not be. He was going to the monastery, but he was not interested in the monastery now; the whole interest was left behind. Then suddenly he remembers that his colleague, another young monk, is coming – they had been on a begging tour. He looks back, and not only is the young monk there, but the young monk is carrying the girl on his shoulders!

This must have created a deep jealousy in the old man. This is what he would like to have done. Because of the rules he couldn't do it. But he must take revenge! They walked in silence for miles, and at the monastery gate the old man suddenly said: "This was not good – this is against the rules."

That silence was false. For all those miles the old man was thinking how to take revenge, how to condemn this young man. He was continuously obsessed; otherwise nothing happens so suddenly, mind is a continuity. For these two or three miles he was continuously thinking what to do, and only now he speaks.

SEX: THE MOST VITAL ENERGY

31

It is not sudden. Inside there has been a current, a running current. And he says: "This is not good, it is against the rules, and I will have to report it to the abbot, to the chief of the monastery, to the master. You have broken a rule, a very basic rule, that no monk should touch a woman. You have not only touched her, you have carried her on your shoulders." The young monk must have felt amazed. So sudden... because there was no girl now, no river, nobody carrying her. The whole thing has happened in the past. For three miles they have been completely silent. And the young monk said: "I left that girl on the bank of the river but you are still carrying her."

This is a deep insight. You can carry things which you are not carrying; you may be burdened by things which are not there; you may be crushed by things which don't exist.

The old monk is on the path of repression. The young monk is a symbol of an effort towards transformation – because transformation accepts the woman, the man, the other. Because transformation has to happen through the other, the other will participate in it. Suppression, repression, rejects the other, is against the other. The other has to be destroyed.

This story is beautiful. The new monk is the way. Don't become the old monks, become the new. Accept life as it is and try to be alert. This young monk must have remained alert while carrying the girl on his shoulders. And if you are alert, what can the girl do?

There is a small anecdote: One monk is leaving Buddha. He is going on a tour to spread the message. So he asks Buddha: "What should I do about women?" That is always the problem with monks. Buddha says: "Don't look at them." This is the simplest way: just close yourself. Don't look at them means just close yourself, forget that they are. Alas, the problem is not so easy. Had it been so easy then all those who know how to close themselves would have been transformed.

One of Buddha's disciples, Ananda, who knows the problem is not so easy.... For Buddha it may look easy. This is a problem: you come with a problem to me; it may be easy for me, but that is not going to help. Ananda knows Buddha has replied casually: Don't look at them. So easy for Buddha! Ananda says. "But it is not so easy. And, Bhagwan," he asks, "if there is a situation where we have to look, if we cannot avoid looking, then what is to be done?" Buddha says: "Don't touch." A look is also a touch – through the eyes. You reach through the eyes and touch. That's why if you stare at a woman for more than three seconds, she will become uneasy. Three seconds is the maximum limit allowed. It is allowed because in life we have to look at each other. But more than three seconds and the woman will become uneasy because you are touching her. Now you are using your eyes as hands. So Buddha says: Don't touch. But Ananda is persistent. Ananda has done such great work for the whole of humanity because he would always persist. He said: "Sometimes there are even situations when we have to touch. What do you say then? If the woman is ill or the woman has fallen in the street and there is nobody else to help and we have to touch. If the situation is such, then what should we do?" Buddha laughs and he says, "Then be alert!"

The last thing Buddha says is the first. Closing the eyes won't help, non-touching won't help – because you can touch in imagination, you can see in imagination. A real woman is not needed, a real man is not needed. Just close your eyes... and you can have an imaginary world of women and men. And you can touch and you can see. Finally, only one thing can help; be alert.

This old monk cannot have heard the whole story, all Buddha's three answers. He remained with the first two. The young monk has understood the thing – be alert. He must have come near the girl.. desire arises... be alert that the desire has arisen. The problem is not the girl, because how can the girl be your problem? She is her problem, not your problem. The desire arises in you, the desire for woman – that is the problem. The girl is not at all the question. Any girl, any woman would do the same. She is just a point of reference. Seeing the girl, the desire has arisen. To be alert means to be alert to this desire, that the desire has come to me.

Now, a man who is on the path of repression will suppress this desire, close his eyes towards the object and run away. That is a run-away method. But where can you run, because you are running from yourself? You can run from the woman who is standing on the riverbank, but you cannot run from the desire that is arising within you. Wherever you go, the desire will be there. Be alert that the desire has arisen. Don't really do anything with the woman. If she asks: "Help me!" – help her. If she says: "I am afraid and I cannot cross this river, carry me on your shoulders" – carry her! She is giving you a golden opportunity to be alert. And be thankful towards her. Just be alert, feel what is arising in you.

What is happening in you? You are carrying the girl, what is happening in you? If you are alert, then there is no woman– only a little weight on your shoulders, that's all. If you are not alert, then there is a woman. If you are alert, then it is just bones, pressing, weight. If you are not alert, then it is all that desire can create, the fantasy, the maya, the illusion. Carrying a girl on your shoulders, both are possible. If you lose alertness for a single moment, suddenly the maya is sitting on your shoulders. If you are alert, just a little weight, that's all... carrying a weight.

This young man crossing the river was passing through a great discipline. Not avoiding the situation that is life – not avoiding life; passing through it with an alert mind. Many times he may have missed. Many times he may have completely forgotten. Then the whole illusion and the maya was there. Many times he may have recaptured his alertness again when suddenly there is light and darkness disappears. But it must have been beautiful to experience this alertness.

Then he dropped the girl on the other bank and started walking towards his monastery, still alert – because it is not a question of whether the woman is there or not: the memory can follow. He may not have enjoyed the woman, her touch, while crossing the river – but he may enjoy it now in the memory. He must have remained alert. He was silent, his silence was true. True silence always comes through alertness. That's why he says: "I have left the girl there, back at the river. I am not carrying her at all. You are still carrying her." In the old monk's mind things are continuing. And he has not done anything, he has not even touched the girl.

So doing is not the question; it is mind, how your mind is functioning. Be alert, and by and by energies are transformed. The old dies and the new is born.

Enough for today.

CHAPTER 2

Religions
Contaminate Sex Energy

Beloved Osho,

Why are all the religions against sex?
And why are you not against sex?

All the religions are against sex because that is the only way to make you miserable. That is the only way to make you feel guilty. That is the only way to reduce you to being sinners.

Sex is one of the most fundamental truths of life, so fundamental that if somebody says it is wrong, he is putting you in trouble. You cannot get rid of it. Unless you become really enlightened you cannot get rid of it. And to become enlightened there is no need to get rid of it. In fact, if you go deeper into it, enlightenment will be easier because a man who has gone deep in love will be capable of going deep in meditation – because in the deepest moments of love there are a few glimpses of meditation.

That's how meditation has been discovered. That's how SAMADHI, *satori* have been discovered. Because in a deep love affair, sometimes, suddenly, your mind disappears. There are no thoughts, no time, no space. You become one with the whole. People have carried those glimpses in their memories and they want to attain to those glimpses more naturally, more in their aloneness, because to depend on the other is not very good, and then it happens only for a moment. How to attain to that glimpse permanently, so it remains there, it becomes your nature?

Religions are against sex because down the centuries they have come to know that sex is the most enjoyable thing for man. So poison his joy. Once you poison his joy and you put this idea in his mind that something is wrong in sex – it is sin – then he will never be able to enjoy it, and if he cannot enjoy it, then his energies will start moving in other directions. He will become more ambitious.

A really sexual person will not be ambitious. Why? He will not hanker to become the prime minister or the president. Why? The energy that becomes ambition is repressed sex. A sexually free person will not try to become anybody. Whatsoever he is, he is beautifully happy. Why should he bother to hoard money...? When you cannot love, you hoard money; money is a substitute. You will never find a money hoarder a loving person, and you will never find a loving person a money hoarder. It is very difficult. Money is a substitute; it is a pseudo love affair. You are afraid to make love to a woman or a man, so you make love to dollars, rupees, pounds. Have you not seen when a miser comes across money? Have you seen the light that comes to his eyes, and how the face becomes luminous, as if he is looking at a beautiful woman or a beautiful man...? Just give him a hundred-dollar note, a greenback, and see how he touches it, how he feels it. Saliva starts flowing. It is a love affair. Just look when he opens his money box and looks into it. He is facing God. Money is his God, his beloved. And when an ambitious person is trying to become the prime minister or the president.... Ambition is sex energy diverted, and the society diverts you. You say, "Why are all the religions against sex?" They are against sex because that is the only way to make you unhappy, guilty, afraid. Once you are afraid, you can be manipulated. Remember this fundamental rule: make a person afraid if you want to dominate him. First make him afraid. If he is afraid, you can dominate him. If he is not afraid, why and how can you dominate him? How will he allow you to be the dominator? He will say, "Be gone. Who are you to dominate me?" First make him afraid.

And there are two things which make people very much afraid. One is death, so religions have exploited that. That you are going to die, that you are going to die, that you are going to die – they persist, so they, they create a trembling. So you say, "What, what am I to do now? How should I behave? How should I live?" And then they say there is hell and there is heaven. Greed and profit, punishment and reward.

So one is death. But death is not yet, so you can postpone it. It is not much of a problem; you say,

"Okay, when we will die we will see. And I am not going to die right now. I am going to live fifty years more, at least, so why bother?" And man does not have a very distant-seeing vision; he does not have radar. He cannot see fifty years ahead. Yes, if you say to him, "Tomorrow you are going to die," he may become afraid, but fifty years? He will say, "Wait, there is no hurry. Let me do my things first." He may even start doing them faster because "Only fifty years are left? So let me do whatsoever I want to do. Eat, drink, be merry."

So the second thing, which is more fear-creating, is sex. Sex is already the problem. Death WILL be the problem; it is in the future. Sex has the problem in the present; it is already there. Religions contaminate your sex energy. They start making you afraid that it is wrong, it is ugly, it is sin, it will drag you to hell. They want to dominate you; that's why they are against sex.

I have no idea to dominate you, I am here to make you absolutely free. And there are only two things needed to make you free. One is that sex is not a sin. Sex is a god-given gift, it is a grace. And second, there is no death. You will be forever, because whatsoever is, remains. Nothing ever disappears. Forms change, names change, but the reality continues. So I take away all fear. I don't want to make you in any way feel guilty, afraid. I want to take all fears from you so that you can live naturally, without any domination, so that you can live according to your own spontaneity.

And that spontaneity will bring enlightenment. Then sex disappears, and then death disappears.

It has disappeared to me, so I know it will disappear to you also. So why be worried...? And it disappears more easily if you have known it rightly. Knowledge of anything takes you beyond; you are finished with it. If you have not lived rightly, you will be as other religious people who have not lived rightly: they hanker, they desire, they dream, but they repress, so they remain clinging to their repressions – they are never free of sex.

A beautiful story. Meditate over it: The time is the not too distant future. We have finally destroyed ourselves by means of a nuclear holocaust. Everyone is waiting restlessly in a seemingly endless line leading up to the gates of heaven. At the head of the line, Peter is deciding which souls shall enter and which shall be turned away.

Some distance from the gates, an American stands in line wringing his hands in apprehension. Suddenly he hears a murmur beginning at the front of the line, and growing into a joyful rush of sound as it builds in volume moving down the line toward his place. He can make out sounds of celebration in many languages. He hears shouts of "Bravo," "Bravissimo," "Bis," "Encore," and "Hip, Hip, Hooray".

"What is it? What is it all about?" he implores of those up ahead of him in the line. At last someone closer to the gates shouts back to him, "Peter just told us, 'Screwing don't count!'..."

Get it? Sex has nothing to do with your enlightenment. Love has nothing to do with your enlightenment. It is in fact going to help you because it will make you more natural. Be natural and don't cultivate any abnormalities, and you will be closer to God.

Hence I am not against sex, I am not against anything. I am only against unnatural attitudes, perverted attitudes. Be natural and normal, and allow God to flow through you. He will take you. His river is already moving towards the sea. Don't try to swim upstream, don't try to push the river. Go with the river. That's what surrender is, and that's what sannyas is.

CHAPTER 3

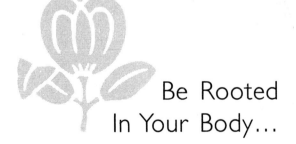

Be Rooted In Your Body…

Beloved Osho,

If man's erotic instincts were liberated, would they not run wild?

First: What is wrong in being wild? I don't see anything wrong in being wild. To be too much civilized may be dangerous – a little wildness is good. And in a better world, with more understanding about human nature, we will keep a balance between civilization and wildness.

We have become very lopsided: we have become just civilized. When you become too civilized you become plastic. The wild rose flower has a beauty – may not be so permanent as the plastic flower, by the evening it may be gone, gone forever, it was only for the moment, but still it is alive. Look at the wild animals – they have something – don't you feel jealous? Don't you feel a radiancy, an aliveness, God more solidly present in them than in you?

So first, I don't see anything wrong in being wild. If your wildness is not destructive to anybody, it is perfectly religious. If your wildness is just your expression of your freedom and it is not in interference with anybody else's freedom, if it is not a trespass on anybody else's life, liberty, it's perfectly good.

In a RIGHT world, people should be allowed all kinds of wildness, with only one condition: that their wildness should not be violent to anybody else. They should be given total freedom. Civilization only has to be negative, it should not be positive. The function of the police and the state has to be negative, it should not be positive. It should not tell you what you should do, it should only tell you what you should not do, that's all. Because we live in a society you cannot be absolutely wild, there are other people. You have to be careful about them too. They are careful about you, they are making compromises for your happiness, you have to make a few compromises for their happiness. But that's all.

The society, the state, the law, should be negative. They should only pinpoint a few things: that which interferes with other people's lives and happiness should not be done. And everything else should be left open. Second thing: Eros is the root of all that is beautiful in the world. The flowers bloom because of eros, and the cuckoos cry because of eros, and the birds dance and sing because of eros. And all that is great and all that is beautiful is because of eros – even samadhi is the ultimate flowering of the energy called eros. God is very erotic. You can see it all around, no proof is needed. The whole existence is erotic.

And the day man started thinking against eros,

man started falling into a kind of abnormality. Since then man has not been normal. And because eros has been crushed, repressed, man has become more and more destructive – because creation comes out of eros. Children are born out of eros, so are paintings, so are songs, so is SAMADHI!

Once you are repressive towards eros, afraid of eros, once you don't worship the god of eros, then what are you going to do? ALL creativity is closed; you become destructive – then wars, violence, aggression, competition, money mania, power politics – they all arise. Man has suffered much because of this stupid attitude about eros. It has given all kinds of perversions.

Somebody is after money. Can't you see the perversion? – money has become the God. He does not love a woman, he loves money instead. Somebody loves his car, and somebody loves power, respectability. These are perversions of eros, and these are the really dangerous people. They should not be there. Genghis Khan and Tamerlaine and Alexander and Adolf Hitler and Stalin and Mao – these are the really dangerous people. These are the people who are destructive. Their joy is destruction. And whenever creative energy is not allowed to have its own say, it turns sour, it becomes bitter, it becomes poisonous.

Man has not suffered from eros, no, not at all. Man has suffered from anti-eros. When you are anti-eros, THANA-TOS – death – becomes your god. Death is worshipped. Money is dead, so is politics, so is ego –

all dead things become very, very important. And you worship these dead idols.

You ask me: IF MAN'S EROTIC INSTINCTS WERE LIBERATED, WOULD THEY NOT RUN WILD?

Maybe, if they were immediately given total freedom, for the time being they may run wild. But that will be only transitory – and the reason is not in eros. The reason will be because for centuries it has been repressed. It is as if a person has been starved for many years. Then you suddenly give him all freedom – you give him the key to the kitchen. Yes, he is going to be wild for a little while, but what is wrong in it? For a few days he is going to eat too much, but only for a few days. He will become obsessively attached to food. He will drink, eat and dream and desire only food and food – only food will float in his mind. But the reason is not hunger: the reason is that you have been starving him. Yes, that's right. And the priests and the popes and the SHANKARACHARYAS they go on saying that eros cannot be given freedom, otherwise people will become just will. But the reason is not in eros, the reason is in the popes. THEY are the sole cause. They have starved humanity for so long, they have crippled humanity for so long – and there is a reason why they have crippled the human eros.

If you want to make human beings slaves, the only way is to destroy their eros. A man whose eros is fully alive is a master. A man whose eros is fully flowering does not bother about anything. He will not be ready to go to any war, to any foolish Vietnam or Korea or anywhere. A man who is really in love with life and enjoying it will not bother about becoming the president or the prime minister of a country. The man who is really living his eros will not even go to the church or to the temple, because he has found the real temple of God. Love is his prayer. Then where will these priests be, and the politicians, and the warmongers, and the people who depend on your obsessions? Your energies have to be destroyed, you have to be set in such a way that you start moving in wrong directions. And a person whose eros has been killed becomes very weak.

That's what you do. Have you not seen a bull and an ox? What is the difference? The erotic freedom of the bull has been destroyed, he becomes an ox. An ox is a poor specimen. A bull is something alive, something divine. In India we worship the bull as divine. He is the bodyguard of Shiva – the bull. Not an ox, remember. An ox would have been far better, more manageable – but the bull.... Why? The bull is so erotic, such a perfect eros; and such beauty exists with the bull. And look at an ox pulling a bullock-cart – a slave. If you want people to be slaves, destroy their eros, pervert their erotic instinct. That's why it has been done up to now.

In the future, eros has to become the religion. Love should be the worship, and the only god that can really be God is eros – because eros is creativity, and we call God the creator.

What is happening to the modern man? What has happened in the past too? You can only be happy when your eros is fulfilled. But there are a thousand and one barriers and it is never fulfilled. You are put in wrong directions and you strive hard. One day you become a great rich man, and you wait and wait for that day when you will be the richest man in the world, and one day you become! But then suddenly you feel there is no joy arising out of it. You were waiting in vain. You were moving a direction where there was no possibility for any joy.

Joy is very simple. If you allow life to flow through you in a natural way, joy is a natural phenomenon. It is spontaneity. It does not wait at the end of your journey – it is here, it is now.

I have heard an anecdote:

An elderly lady was sitting in her rocking chair knitting, her Persian cat reclining at her feet. Suddenly a fairy appeared and asked the old lady if there was anything she wished.

"Yes," was the reply, "I would like to be a young woman again."

The fairy waved her wand – and there she stood, a lovely girl of eighteen!

"Now," asked the fairy, "is there any other wish you would like granted?"

"Oh, yes, I would like a handsome young man."

Turning to the cat, the fairy waved her wand, in its place rose a fine looking youth.

He looked sadly at the girl and sighed, "Now aren't you sorry you took me to the vet?"

That's what is happening – humanity is castrated. So you can have money but you will not have joy. You can have power but you will not have joy; you can have respectability but you will not have joy. Joy arises out of eros. And the last thing I would like to tell you: It is only through eros that eros is transcended, never otherwise. It is only through eros that one day you transcend it. ANYTHING THAT HAS BEEN LIVED TOTALLY IS ALWAYS TRANSCENDED. Hang-ups simply mean that you have not lived something totally. So people WHO have not lived their eros, have been afraid, will remain confined to it. Their sex will become cerebral. It may disappear from their bodies but it will remain in their heads –which is not a right place for it! People who have lived their sexual lives naturally, with no inhibition and no taboo, one day come to a point where it simply disappears – not through fight, but through understanding. A transcendence comes, and that is BRAHMACHARYA.

BRAHMACHARYA is the ultimate fragrance of eros. It is NOT against eros; it is the ultimate fragrance of eros. It is the subtlest eros. One is so much in tune with one's erotic energy that the man does not need the woman and the woman does not need the man. One is so enough unto oneself, one has discovered one's own inner woman by and by. Looking into many women's eyes, one has come to feel one's own inner woman. Looking into many other men's eyes, being with many men, going deep into their being, looking into their mirror, finding oneself, one has found one's inner man. And remember, man is both woman and man; woman is both man and woman. We carry both inside. There comes a point where our inner woman and inner man meet. In Tantra we call it YOGA NADHA.

You must have seen a tremendously significant statue of Shiva, ARDHARNARISHWAR – half is man and half is woman. Shiva is depicted half as man and half as woman. That is the ultimate meeting, the real orgasm, the cosmic orgasm. When it has happened one becomes a BRAHMACHARIN, one attains to real celibacy. That is ultimate virginity: no need for the other; the need for the other has disappeared.

CHAPTER 4

Brahmacharya:
The Ultimate Fragrance
Of Eros

Beloved Osho,

I love my husband but I hate sex, and that
creates conflict. Isn't sex animalistic?

I t is. But man is an animal – as much of an animal
as any other animal. But when I say that man is an
animal, I don't mean that man finishes with animality;
he can be more than the animal, he can be less also.
That is the glory of man, the freedom and the danger,
the agony and the ecstasy. A man can be far lower than
animals, and a man can be far higher than gods. Man
has infinite potentiality.

A dog is a dog; he remains a dog. He is born a dog
and he will die a dog. A man can become a Buddha,
and a man can become an Adolf Hitler too. So man is
very open-ended on both sides – he can fall back. Can
you find any animal more dangerous than man, more
mad than man? Just think of a scene: fifty thousand
monkeys sitting in a stadium killing small children –
throwing them into a fire. What will you think about
them? Thousands of children are being thrown into
a fire... A great fire is burning just in the middle of
the stadium, and fifty thousand monkeys enjoying

with joy, dancing, and children are being thrown – their own children. What will you think about these monkeys? Will you not think that the monkeys have gone mad? But this has happened in humanity. In Carthage it happened: fifty thousand men burning children. They burnt three hundred children at one time. As an offering to their god. Their own children! But forget about Carthage, it is long past. What did Adolf Hitler do in this century? Of course, this is a far-advanced century, so Adolf Hitler was capable of doing greater things than Carthage. He killed millions of Jews, thousands at a time would be forced into a chamber and gassed. And hundreds of people would be looking from the outside... watching through one-way mirrors. What you will think about these people? What type of men...? People being gassed, burnt, evaporated, and others are watching? Can you think about animals doing such a thing?

During three thousand years, man has been through five thousand wars – killing and killing and killing. And you call sex animalistic? Animals have never done anything more "animalistic" than man. And you think man is not an animal?

Man IS an animal. And the idea that man is not an animal is one of the hindrances for your growth. So you take it for granted that you are not animals, and then you stop growing. The first recognition has to be this: "I am an animal and I have to be alert and go beyond it."

It happened:

A man wrote to a country hotel in Ireland to
ask if his dog would be allowed to stay there.
He received the following answer: Dear Sir, I
have been in the hotel business for over thirty
years. Never yet have I had to call in the police
to eject a disorderly dog in the small hours of
the morning. No dog has ever attempted to
pass off a bad cheque on me. Never has a dog
set the bed-clothes alight through smoking.
I have never found a hotel towel in a dog's
suitcase. Your dog is welcome P.S. If he can
vouch for you, you can come too!

Animals are beautiful, whatsoever they are; they are
just innocent. Man is very cunning, very calculating,
very ugly. Man can fall lower than the animals, because
man can rise higher than man, higher than gods. Man
has an infinite potentiality: he can be the lowest and
he can be the highest. He has the whole ladder, in his
being, from the first rung to the last rung. So the first
thing I would like to say to you, don't call sex just
animalistic, because sex can be just animalistic – that
is possible, but it need not be. It can rise higher, it can
become love, it can become prayer. It depends on you.

Sex in itself is nothing like a fixed entity; it is just
a possibility. You can make it as you like it, as you
want it. That is the whole message of Tantra: that sex

can become SAMADHI. That is the vision of Tantra: that sex can become SAMADHI, that through sex the ultimate ecstasy can enter in you. Sex can become the bridge between you and the ultimate.

You say: I LOVE MY HUSBAND BUT I HATE SEX, AND THAT CREATES CONFLICT. How can you love your husband and yet hate sex? You must be playing on words. How can you love your husband and hate sex?

Just try to understand it. When you love a man, you would like to hold his hand too. When you love a man, you would like to hug him sometimes too. When you love a man, you would not only like to hear his sound, you would like to see his face too. When you only hear the sound of your beloved, the beloved is far away, the sound is not enough; when you see him too you are more satisfied. When you touch him, certainly you are more satisfied. When you taste him, certainly you are even more satisfied. What is sex? It is just a meeting of two deep energies.

You must be carrying some taboos in your mind, inhibitions. What is sex? Just two person meeting at the maximum point – not only holding hands, not only hugging each other's bodies, but penetrating into each other's energy realm. Why should you hate sex? Your mind must have been conditioned by the MAHATMAS, the so-called "religious" people who have poisoned the whole of humanity, who have poisoned your very source of growth. Why should you hate? If you love your man, you would like to share your total being with him: there is no need to hate. And if you hate sex, what are you saying? You are simply saying that you want the man to take care of you financially, to take care of the house, to bring you a car and a fur coat. You want to use the man... and you call it love? And you don't want to share anything with him.

When you love, you share all. When you love, you don't have any secrets. When you love, you have your heart utterly open; you are available. When you love, you are ready to go with him even to hell if he is going to hell. But this happens. We are very expert with words: we don't want to say that we don't love, so we make it look as if we love and we hate sex. Sex is not all love – that's true, love is more than sex – that's true; but sex is the very foundation of it. Yes, one day sex disappears, but to hate it is not the way to make it disappear. To hate it is the way to repress it. And whatsoever is repressed will come up one way or other. Please don't try to become a monk or a nun.

Listen to this story:

The nuns ran an orphanage, and one day the Mother Superior summoned to her office three buxom girls who were leaving and said: "Now, you are all going out into the big sinful world and I must warn you against certain men. There are men who will buy you drinks, take you to a room, undress you and do unspeakable things to you. Then they give you two or three pounds, and you're sent away, ruined!"

"Excuse me, Reverend Mother," said the boldest one, "did you say these wicked men do this to us and give us three pounds too?"

"Yes, dear child. Why do you ask?"

"Well, the priests only give us apples."

Remember, sex is natural. One can go beyond it, but not through repression. And if you repress it, sooner or later you will find some other way to express it; some perversion is bound to enter – you will have to find some substitute. And substitutes are of NO help at all; they DON'T help, they CAN'T help. And once a natural problem has been turned in such a way that you have forgotten about it, and it has bubbled up somewhere else as a substitute, you can go on fighting with the substitute, but it is not going to help.

I have heard...

A stranger got into a suburban railway carriage in which two men were already sitting. One of them had a peculiar mannerism – he scratched his elbow again and again and again. This elbow-scratching was nearly driving the stranger mad by the time the victim got out at his station. "Gravely afflicted, your friend," he said to the other man. "Yes, indeed. He has got a terrible dose of piles."

"I'm not talking about piles. I'm talking about all that scratching just now." "Yes, that is right – piles. You see he is a very religious man and a civil servant too. And that scratching of the elbow is just a substitute."

But substitutes never help; they only create perversions. Obsessions. Be natural if you want to go beyond nature some day. Be natural: that is the first requirement. I am not saying that there is nothing more than nature, there is a higher nature – that is the whole message of Tantra. But be very earthly if you really want to rise high in the sky.

Can't you see these trees? They are rooted in the earth, and the better they are rooted the higher they go. The higher they want to go, the deeper they will have to go into the earth. If a tree wants to touch the stars, the tree will have to go and touch the very hell – that's the only way. Be rooted in your body if you want to become a soul. Be rooted in your sex if you really want to become a lover. Yes, the more energy is converted into love, the less and less need of sex will be there, but you will not hate it.

Hate is not a right relationship with anything. Hate simply shows that you are afraid. Hate simply shows that there is great fear in you. Hate simply shows that deep down you are still attracted. If you hate sex, then your energy will start moving somewhere else. Energy has to move. Man, if he suppresses sex, becomes more ambitious. If you really want to be ambitious you have to suppress sex. Then only can ambition have energy, otherwise you will not have any energy. A politician has to suppress sex, then only can he rush towards New Delhi. Sex energy is needed. Whenever you are suppressing sex, you are angry at the whole world; you can become a great revolutionary. All revolutionaries are bound to be sexually repressed. When, in a better world, sex will be simple, natural, accepted without any taboo and without any inhibition, politics will disappear and there will be no revolutionaries, there will be no need. When a man represses sex, he becomes too attached to money; he has to put his sexual energy somewhere. Have you not seen people holding their hundred rupee notes as if they were touching their beloved? Can't you see in their eyes the same lust? But this is ugly. To hold a woman with deep love is beautiful; to hold a hundred rupee note with lust is just ugly – it is a substitute.

You cannot deceive animals...

A man went to the zoo and took his son; he wanted to show his son the monkeys there. The son was very interested: he had never seen monkeys. They went there – but no monkeys. So he asked the zoo-keeper, "What has happened? Where are the monkeys?"

And the zoo-keeper said, "This is their love season, so they have gone into the hut."

The man was very frustrated. For months he had been trying to bring the boy. They had travelled far, and now this was love season! So he asked, "If we throw nuts won't they come out?" And the zoo-keeper said, "Would you?"

But I think man can come out; if you throw nuts, man HAS to come out. The zoo-keeper is wrong: the monkeys will not come that is certain; if you give them money they will not come. They will say, "Keep your money. The love season is on! Keep your money."

And if you say, "We can make you President of India", they will say, "You keep your presidency. The love season is on!"

But man, if you make him a president, can kill his beloved. If that is the stake, he can do that. These are substitutes. You cannot befool animals.

I have heard...

The spinster had a parrot who kept repeating "I want to poke! I want to poke!" She found this slightly irritating, until a married friend explained what it meant. Then she became very alarmed...."
"I love that bird, but I'll have to get rid of him, or the vicar will never call again" she said. But her more experienced friend said, "Well, if you really

love him, you'll get him what he longs for, which is a female, then he won't keep on about it all the time."

Off went the spinster to the bird shop, but the man said,

"No can do, no lady parrots coming in all season, Miss. But I can do you a lady owl at a reasonable price."

Anything was better than nothing, so she popped the owl into the parrot's cage, and waited with thrilled anticipation...

"I want to poke! I want to poke!" said the parrot.

"Ooo-Ooo." said the lady owl.

"Not you, you goggle-eyed freak!" said the parrot, "I can't stand women who wear glasses!"

Substitutes won't do. Man is living with substitutes. Sex is natural, money is unnatural. Sex is natural; power, prestige, respectability are unnatural. If you really want to hate something, hate money, hate power, hate prestige. Why hate love?

Sex is one of the most beautiful phenomena in the world. Of course, the lowest, that is true, but the higher moves through the lower – the lotus comes out of the mud. Don't hate the mud, otherwise how will you help the mud to release the lotus? Help the mud, take care of the mud, so that the lotus is released.

Certainly, the lotus is so far away from the mud that you cannot even conceive of any relationship. If you see a lotus, you cannot believe that it comes out of dirty mud. But it comes: it is the expression of the dirty mud.

The soul is released from the body. Love is released from sex. Sex is a body thing, love is a spiritual thing. Sex is like mud, love is like a lotus. But without the mud the lotus is not possible, so don't hate the mud. The whole Tantra message is simple; it is very scientific and it is very natural. The message is that if you really want to go beyond the world, go into the world DEEPLY, fully alert, aware.

CHAPTER 5

Key To Eternal Life

Beloved Osho,

Isn't tantra a way of indulgence?

It is not. It is the ONLY way to get out of indulgence. It is the only way to get out of sexuality. No other way has ever been helpful for man; all other ways have made man more and more sexual.

Sex has not disappeared. The religions have made it only more poisoned. It is still there – in a poisoned form. Yes, guilt has arisen in man, but sex has not disappeared. It CANNOT disappear because it is a biological-reality. It is existential; it cannot simply disappear by repressing it. It can disappear only when you become so alien that you can release the energy encapsulated in sexuality – not by repression is the energy released, but by understanding. And once the energy is released, out of the mud the lotus.... The lotus has to come UP out of the mud, it has to go higher, and repression takes it deeper into the mud. It goes on repressing it.

What you have done up to now, the whole humanity, is repressing sex in the mud of the unconscious. Go on repressing it, sit on top of it; don't allow it to move;

kill it by fasting, by discipline, by going to a cave in the Himalayas, by moving to a monastery where a woman is not allowed. There are monasteries where a woman has never entered for hundreds of years; there are monasteries where only nuns have lived and a man has never entered. These are ways of repressing. AND they create more and more sexuality and more and more dreams of indulgence.

No, Tantra is not a way of indulgence. It is the only way of freedom. Tantra says: Whatsoever is has to be understood and through understanding changes occur of their own accord.

So listening to me or listening to Saraha, don't start thinking that Saraha is supporting your indulgence. You will be in bad shape if you accept that. Listen to this story:

An elderly gent named Martin went to a doctor for an examination. "I want you to tell me what's wrong, doctor. I feel some pains here and there, and I can't understand it. I've lived a very clean life – no smoking, drinking or running around. I'm in bed, alone, at nine o'clock every night. Why should I feel this way?"

"How old are you?" asked the doctor.

"I'll be seventy-four on my next birthday," said Martin. The doctor answered, "After all, you're getting on in years, you've got to expect things like that. But you've lots of time left yet. Just take it easy, and don't worry. I suggest you go to Hot Springs."

So Martin went to Hot Springs. There he met another gent who looked so old and decrepit that Martin felt encouraged by the comparison. "Brother," says Martin, "you sure must have taken good care of yourself, living to such a ripe old age. I've lived a quiet, clean life, but not like you, I'll bet. What is your formula for obtaining a ripe old age like you have reached?" So this shriveled old guy says, "On the contrary, sir. When I was seventeen my father told me, 'Son, you go and enjoy life. Eat, drink and be merry to your heart's content. Live life to the fullest. Instead of marrying one woman, be a bachelor and have ten. Spend your money for fun, for yourself, instead of on a wife and kids.' Yeah: wine, women and song, life lived to the full. That's been my policy all my life, brother!"

"Sounds like you got something," said Martin. "How old are you?" The other answered, "Twenty-four."

Indulgence is suicidal – as suicidal as repression. These are the two extremes that Buddha says to avoid. One extreme is repression, the other extreme is indulgence. Just be in the middle; neither be repressive, nor be indulgent. Just be in the middle, watchful, alert, aware. It is your life! Neither does it have be repressed, nor does it have to be wasted – it has to be understood.

It is your life – take care of it! Love it! Befriend it! If you can befriend your life, it will reveal many mysteries to you, it will take you to the very door of God.

But Tantra is not indulgence at all. The repressive people have always thought that Tantra is indulgence; their minds are so much obsessed. For example: a man who goes to a monastery and lives there without ever seeing a woman, how can he believe that Saraha is not indulging when he lives with a woman? Not only lives but practises strange things: sitting before the woman naked, the woman is naked, and he goes on watching the woman; or even while making love to the woman he goes on watching.

Now, you cannot watch his watching; you can see only that he is making love to a woman. And if you are repressive, your whole repressed sexuality will bubble up. You must start going mad! And you will project all that you have repressed in yourself on Saraha –and Saraha is not doing anything like that; he is moving in a totally different dimension. He is not really interested in the body: he wants to see what this sexuality is; he wants to see what this appeal of orgasm is; he wants to see what exactly orgasm is; he wants to be meditative in that peak moment, so that he can find the clue and the key... maybe there is the key to open the door of the Divine. In fact, it is there.

God has hidden the key in your sexuality. On the one hand, through your sex, life survives; that is only partial use of your sex energy. On another hand, if you move with full awareness in your sex energy, you will find that you have come across a key that can help you to enter into eternal life. One small aspect of sex is that your children will live. The other aspect, a higher aspect, is that you can live in eternity. Sex energy is life energy.

Ordinarily we don't move further than the porch, we never go into the palace. Saraha is trying to go into the palace. Now, the people who came to the king, they must have been suppressed people as all people are suppressed. The politician and the priest HAVE to teach suppression, because it is only through suppression that people are driven insane. And you can rule insane people more easily than sane people. And when people are insane in their sex energy, they start moving in other directions – they will start moving towards money, or power, or prestige. They have to show their sex energy somewhere or other; it is boiling there – they have to release it in some way or other. So money-madness or power-addiction, they become their releases.

This whole society is sex-obsessed. If sex-obsession disappears from the world, people will not be money-mad. Who will bother about money? And people will not be bothered by power. Nobody will like to become a president or a prime minister – for what?

Life is so tremendously beautiful in its ordinariness, it is so superb in its ordinariness, why should one want to become somebody? By being nobody it is so delicious – nothing is missing. But if you destroy people's sexuality and make them repressed, so much is missing that they are always hankering: somewhere there must be joy – here it is missing.

Sex is one of the activities given by nature and God in which you are thrown again and again to the present moment. Ordinarily you are never in the present – except when you are making love, and then too for a few seconds only.

Tantra says one has to understand sex, to decode sex. If sex is so vital that life comes out of it, then there must be something more to it. That something more is the key towards Divinity, towards God.

CHAPTER 6

Alchemy Of
Transformation

Beloved Osho,

What is the difference between sexual power and sexual energy?

Sexual energy is another name for your life force. The word "sex" has become condemned by the religions; otherwise there is nothing wrong in it. It is your very life. Sexual energy is a natural energy: you are born out of it. It is your creative energy. When the painter paints or the poet composes or the musician plays or the dancer dances, these are all expressions of your life force.

Not only are children born out of your sexual energy, but everything that man has created on the earth has come out of sexual energy. Sexual energy can have many transformations: at the lowest it is biological; at the highest it is spiritual. It has to be understood that all creative people are highly sexual. You can see the poets, you can see the painters, you can see the dancers. All creative people are highly sexual, and the same is true about the people whom I call the mystics. Perhaps they are the most sexual people on the earth, because they are so full of life energy, abundant, overflowing....

But sexual power is a totally different thing. Sexual power is politics. It is using your sex to dominate people. Domination can be done in many ways: somebody dominates because he has money, somebody dominates because he has more physical strength, somebody dominates because he has more knowledge, somebody dominates because he is clever enough to befool people and collect their votes, somebody can dominate through her or his sexual power. More often it is the woman's way to dominate.

The woman can dominate because of her sexual appeal, but it is ugly and mean. It is selling your body just to dominate.

One of the most beautiful women in the world was Cleopatra. She was a queen in Egypt. Her country never went into war; whenever there was an attack, she herself would go and offer her body to the invader, to the leader of the armies – and she had such beauty that she easily persuaded the general of the army. She seduced the general by giving her body. She was using her power – her sex, her beauty, her charm – and she remained the queen of Egypt without ever taking her armies to fight with anybody. A very strange woman....

But all women in different degrees dominate through their sex. They use it as a power. To use sex as a power is to degrade oneself, is to lose one's dignity and self-respect. It is pure prostitution.

The difference between British and French girls is this: they both know what men like, but the French girl does not mind.

> Business was brisk for the pretty young prostitute in the bar. "Bill," she said, "you can come over about seven-ish, and you, George around eight-ish, and Frank, I will have time for you about nine-ish." She then looked around the crowded bar and called out, "Anyone for ten-ish?"

Using your sexual energy as a profession, selling it as a commodity may give you a certain feeling of power, but you are destroying yourself by your own hands. Sexual energy is not to be used as a political means. Sexual energy is your potentiality for spiritual growth. You can become enlightened only because of your sexual energy.

I have been searching for almost thirty-five years, in all kinds of books, strange scriptures from Tibet and Ladakh and China and Japan — India has the greatest number of scriptures in the world — and I have been looking for one thing: has there ever been an enlightened impotent person? There is no incidence recorded anywhere. An impotent person has never been a great poet either, or a great singer, or a great sculptor, or a great scientist. What is the problem with the impotent person? He has no life force; he is hollow. He cannot create anything – and to create oneself as an enlightened being needs tremendous energy.

Never use your sex as a commodity; as a strategy to dominate, because you are committing suicide. You are destroying the power that can take you to the highest peak of consciousness.

Robert, an American, had been in Italy during the war and had made friends with Giovanni. A few years later he went back to Rome to visit his friend. As soon as Giovanni saw Bob, he could not do enough for him. He showed him the sights and then took him out for a beautiful meal of finest spaghetti.

After the meal, Giovanni insisted that Bob meet his sister.

"Is she pretty?" asked Bob.

"Bella! Bella!" cried Giovanni.

"Is she young?" continued Bob.

"Si! Si!" cried Giovanni.

"And is she pure?" asked Bob.

"My god!" said Giovanni, "you Americans really are crazy!"

Sex has become a thing of the marketplace. On the one hand, religions have been repressing sexual energy and creating perversions which have culminated in the dangerous disease AIDS, which has no cure. The whole credit goes to religions, and if they have any sense of being human, then all the churches and all the monasteries and the Vatican itself should be turned into hospitals for the people suffering from AIDS, because these are the people who have created them. Theirs is the responsibility. They have forced men to live separately from women; they have insisted that celibacy is the very foundation of a religious life. But celibacy is unnatural, and anything unnatural cannot be the foundation of a religious life. Because celibacy is unnatural, and religions have divided men and women into different monasteries, they have created the situation for homosexuality. They are the pioneers of homosexuality; and homosexuality has led to AIDS, which cannot be called simply a disease because it does not come in the category of diseases. It is death itself.

So on the one hand religions have created perversions; on the other hand they insisted on monogamy, which in fact means monotony. That has created the profession of the prostitute. The priest is responsible for the prostitute. It is so ugly and sick that we have created objects, commodities, things to be exploited out of so many beautiful women. Even today, it is not understood exactly what sex is. It need not be repressed, because it is your very energy. It has to be transformed certainly; it has to be raised to its highest purity.

And as you start moving upwards... the name of the ladder is meditation... sex becomes love, sex becomes compassion, and ultimately sex becomes the explosion of your inner being, the illumination, the awakening, the enlightenment. But it is sexual energy.... it can rot, it can go into perversions. But if it is to be understood naturally and helped through meditation to move upwards towards silent spaces, to pass through your heart and reach to the seventh center at the highest point in your body... you will feel grateful towards the energy. Right now you feel only ashamed. This shame and guilt is created by the religious organizations, founders of religion. Naturally the question arises, why did they make sex a mess? And through making a mess of sex they have messed up the whole world and its mind and its growth. Why? – because this was the simplest way to keep humanity in slavery. This was the simplest way to keep people guilty, and anybody who feels guilty can never raise his head in revolt. So all the vested interests wanted man to lose his dignity, self-respect, to feel guilty, ashamed. They have been condemning sex continuously, and their condemnation has led the whole world into a very miserable, psychologically abnormal state. And they are still doing their work.... Just the other day, one Shankaracharya, Jayendra Saraswati, has given a statement that no religious man can support family planning – and all religions will agree with the Hindu Shankaracharya. But I am puzzled. The Christian God has only one begotten son: if that is not family planning, then what is it? The Hindu God Shiva has only two sons: if that is not family planning, then what is it?

To say that no religious person can support family planning is simply madness. The world has already become over-populated because of these religious people. By the end of this century almost half of humanity will have to die through starvation – and who will be responsible for it? These religious people who are not in favor of family planning.

I would like to contradict Shankaracharya Jayendra Saraswati: without any exception, absolutely anyone who is religious is bound to support family planning. And those who don't support it are not religious; they are cunning politicians. They want the world to remain poor, they want the world to be always in a state of begging, so rich people can enjoy donations and can make reservations in paradise by those donations. If there is nobody poor in the world, who is going to accept their donations? The politicians want people to remain starving because starving people are very obedient; they don't have the energy to revolt, to be disobedient. Nobody is concerned with humanity; everybody is concerned with his own power. And still in this century, when things are coming to such a great crisis, a Shankaracharya – who is the equivalent of a pope to the Hindus – declares that family planning is against religion. Then starvation and millions of people dying through hunger seems to be religious, seems to be the will of God, who is called love, who is called compassionate. What kind of compassion is this? But these religious people are more interested in the numbers; Jayendra Saraswati is interested in numbers. Hindu society should not follow any birth control methods, because if they follow birth control methods then their numbers will shrink – and Christians will go on growing bigger and bigger. It is politics of numbers. Mohammedans insist that they should be allowed to have four wives, without any consideration that in existence there is a certain balance, an equal number of women and men. If a man is allowed to have four wives, what about the three men who will be deprived of women? They are bound to go to the prostitutes, they are bound to become homosexuals, they are bound to practice sodomy.

All these crimes are perpetuated by your so-called virtuous leaders, religious saints. But they have been doing this harm for thousands of years. Rather than helping man to sublimate his energies, to make them creative, they have only been able to force man to repress his energies. And repressed energies become a cancer, repressed energies create all kinds of perversions.

The teacher asked her children's art class to draw on the blackboard their impressions of the most exciting thing they could think of.

Little Hymie got up and drew a long jagged line.

"What is that?" asked the teacher.

"Lightning," said Hymie. "Every time I see lightning I get so excited, I scream."

"Very good," said the teacher.

Next, little Sally drew a long wavy line. She explained that it was the sea which always excited her. The teacher thought that was excellent too.

Then little Ernie came up to the blackboard, made a single dot and sat down.

"What is that?" asked the puzzled teacher.

"It is a period," said Ernie.

"Well," said the teacher, "what is so exciting about a period?"

"I don't know," said Ernie to the teacher, "but my sister has missed two of them and my whole family is excited."

This excitement has made the whole world a mad asylum, and it goes on growing so fast that it always defeats all scientific calculations. Just forty years ago, when India became free, it had four hundred million people. Now, after only forty years, it has nine hundred million people. Five hundred million people have been produced in forty years; and by the end of this century, the calculations of the scientists are that it will be the biggest nation in the world for the first time – up to now China has been the first – it will go beyond one billion people. And Jayendra Saraswati is talking about no family planning, no birth control.... Is this country capable of managing one billion people? – their food, their clothes, their education, their medicine? It will not be even able to provide them with drinking water. Food is impossible; even today, half the population of India sleeps hungry in the night because they cannot afford more than one meal a day.

I have seen people who have not been able to find even one meal a day. Then sleep is very difficult: your stomach is turning, asking for food, it is aching, it is painful. With my own eyes I have seen people putting a brick on their stomach and tying it around the waist, just to feel some weight, because inside the stomach there is nothing. These people suffering in misery are the responsibility of people like Shankaracharya Jayendra Saraswati – these are the criminals.

When one thousand people were dying per day in Ethiopia, even then the Pope was continuously talking about no birth control, Mother Teresa was talking about no birth control. You have to see the implications: Mother Teresa needs orphans; without orphans she does not have any qualifications to have a Nobel prize. But from where can you get orphans if birth control methods are applied? And strangely enough, they condemn birth control methods because they are not God's creation, but they don't condemn medicine, which is also not God's creation. At least there is no mention of medicine in those six days when he made the world.

Medicine has given man longer life. There are people in the Soviet Union who have passed their one hundred and eightieth year, and they are still young; there is every possibility that they will pass their second century. There are thousands who have passed beyond one hundred and fifty... and no religious leader condemns it, saying that medicine should be stopped from giving people health and longevity. No religious leader goes on saying that diseases should be allowed because they are God-created.

Medicine can be used; people can be made more healthy... and naturally when they are more healthy they are more sexually powerful. But birth control methods cannot be used because they will reduce the numbers of their congregations. It is a competition of numbers.

Catholics are six hundred million in number. It is the greatest religion in the world – only because of the numbers; otherwise it is the most third-rate religion in the world, there is nothing much in it which can be called religious. But it is the biggest religion, the greatest religion, only on the strength of numbers.

It cannot allow numbers to decline – even if these numbers are going to kill the whole of humanity.

I am in absolute favor of birth control methods for two reasons: birth control methods will keep the world healthy, nourished; secondly, once birth control methods are used, sex loses its profanity – or its sacredness. It becomes simple fun, it becomes just a joyful exchange of energies. According to me, the birth control pill is the greatest invention that man has made. It is the greatest revolution because it can make man and woman equal, liberated. Otherwise the woman is constantly pregnant, and because of her pregnancy she cannot be independent financially, she cannot be independent educationally, she cannot be independent from man's domination. Once she is free from being pregnant compulsorily she will have as much time, as much energy to be creative. Until now half of humanity has remained uncreative... no great poets, no great saints, no great musicians, no great artists. Women have had no time. I was surprised to know that even the books on cookery are written by men, not by women. And the best cooks are men, not women: in all the great five-star hotels you will find great cooks, always men. Strange.... That has been the domain of the woman forever, but she has no energy left. Because of these religious people, she will never be liberated.

Sex energy has to be welcomed and transformed through the alchemy of meditation into higher states of being, into creativity in different dimensions, not only creating more and more children. Life has to be planned, it should not be accidental.

I have heard that when God was making the world, he called man aside and gave him twenty years of normal sex life. Man was horrified: "Only twenty years?!" he cried. But God would not budge. That was all he would give him. Then God called the monkey and gave him twenty years. "But, God! I don't need that much," said the monkey, "ten is enough."

Man spoke up and said, "Can I have the other ten?" – and the monkey agreed. Then God called the lion and gave him twenty years. The lion, too, only wanted ten. Again the man said, "Can I have the other ten?"

The lion roared, "Of course!"

Then came the donkey. He was given twenty years, but he also only wanted ten. Man asked for the extra ten, and got them.

This explains why man has twenty years of a normal sex life, then ten years of monkeying around, ten years of lion about it, and ten years of making an ass of himself.

CHAPTER 7

Sex And Money : A Deep Association

Beloved Master,

Why do I always feel that sex and money are somehow deeply connected with each other?

Nirmal, they are connected. Money is power; hence it can be used in many ways. It can purchase sex, and down the ages that has been the case. Kings have been keeping thousands of wives. Just in this century, the twentieth century, just thirty years ago, forty years ago, the Nizam of Hyderabad had five hundred wives!

It is said that Krishna had sixteen thousand wives. I used to think that this was too much, but when I came to know that the Nizam of Hyderabad had five hundred wives just forty years ago, then it doesn't seem too much – only thirty-two times more! It seems humanly possible. If you can manage five hundred, why not sixteen thousand?

All the kings of the world were doing that. Women were used like cattle. In the great kings' palaces the women were numbered. It was difficult to remember names, so the king could say to his servants, "Bring number four hundred and one" – because how to remember five hundred names? Numbers... just as soldiers are numbered; they don't have names but only numbers. And it makes a lot of difference.

Numbers are absolutely mathematical. Numbers don't breathe, they don't have any heart. Numbers don't have any soul. When a soldier dies in the war, on the notice board you simply read, "Number 15 died." Now, "Number 15 died" is one thing; if you say exactly the name of the person, that is totally different. Then he was a husband and the wife will be a widow now; he was a father and the children will be orphans now; he was the only support of his old parents, now there will be no support. A family is deserted, the light of a family has disappeared. But when number fifteen dies, number fifteen has no wife, remember; number fifteen doesn't have any children, number fifteen doesn't have any old parents. Number fifteen is just number fifteen! And number fifteen is replaceable – another person will come and will become number fifteen. But no individual human being is replaceable. It is a trick, a psychological trick, to give numbers to soldiers. It helps... nobody takes any note of numbers disappearing; new numbers go on coming and replacing the old numbers.

Wives were numbered, and it depended on how much money you had. In fact, in the old days, that was the only way to know how rich a man was; it was a kind of measurement. How many wives has he?

Now, Hindus, particularly ARYA SAMAJIS, criticize Hazrat Mohammed very much for having nine wives – and they don't think of Krishna who had sixteen thousand wives. And he is not an exception, he is the rule. In this country, as in other countries, down the ages, the woman has been exploited – and the way to exploit is money! The whole world has suffered through prostitution, it degrades human beings. And what is a prostitute? She has been reduced to a mechanism, and you can purchase her with money. But remember perfectly well that your wives are not very different either. A prostitute is like a taxi, and your wife is like your own car, it is a permanent arrangement. Poor people cannot make permanent arrangements, they have to use taxis. Rich people can make permanent arrangements – they can have their own cars. And the richer they are, the more cars they can have. I know one person who had three hundred and sixty-five cars – one car for every day. And he had one car made in solid gold....

Money is power, and power can purchase anything. So, Nirmal, you are not wrong that there is some connection between sex and money. One thing more has to be understood. The person who represses sex becomes more money-minded, because money becomes a substitute for sex. Money becomes his love. See the greedy person, the money maniac: the way he touches hundred-rupee notes – he touches them as if he is caressing his beloved; the way he looks at gold, look at his eyes – so romantic. Even great poets will feel inferior. Money has become his love, his goddess. In India, people even worship money. There is a particular day to worship money – actual money – notes and coins, rupees, they worship. Intelligent people doing such stupid things!

Sex can be diverted in many ways. It can become anger if repressed. Hence the soldier has to be deprived of sex, so that the sex energy becomes his anger, his irritation, his destructiveness so he can be more violent than he ever was. Sex can be diverted into ambition. Repress sex: once sex is repressed, you have energy available, you can channel it into any direction. It can become a search for political power, it can become a search for more money, it can become a search for fame, name, respectability, asceticism, etcetera.

Man has only one energy – that energy is sex. There are not many energies within you. And only the one energy has been used for all kinds of drives. It is a tremendously potential energy.

People are after money in the hope that when they have more money, they can have more sex. They can have far more beautiful women or men, they can have far more variety. Money gives them freedom of choice.

The person who is free of sexuality, whose sexuality has become a transformed phenomenon, is also free of money, is also free of ambition, is also free of the desire to be famous. Immediately all these things disappear from his life. The moment sex energy starts rising upwards, the moment sex energy starts becoming love, prayer, meditation, then all lower manifestations disappear.

But sex and money are deeply associated. Your idea, Nirmal, has some truth in it.

A wizened little client in a fancy whorehouse is heard shouting from the upper floor: "No! Not that way! I want it my way, the way we do it in Brooklyn. So quit it! Do it my way or forget it!"

The madam climbs the stairs and erupts into the girl's room. "What is the matter with you, Zelda?" she says. "Give it to him his way."

She leaves, the girl lies down, and the man makes love to her in perfectly routine fashion. She sits up, puts on her dressing gown, lights a cigarette and says, "That's your way, Hymie, huh?"

"That's it," he says proudly from the bed.

"That's how you do it in Brooklyn?"

"Right you are!"

"So what is so different about it?"

"In Brooklyn I get it for nothing."

People can be so obsessed with money, as much as they are obsessed with sex. The obsession can be shifted towards money. But money gives you purchasing power and you can purchase anything. You cannot purchase love, of course, but you can purchase sex. Sex is a commodity, love is not. You cannot purchase prayer, but you can purchase priests. Priests are commodities – prayer is not a commodity. And that which can be purchased is ordinary, mundane. That which cannot be purchased is sacred. Remember it: the sacred is beyond money, the mundane is always within money's power. And sex is the most mundane thing in the world.

A man enters a modern Chicago whorehouse-
night-club run by the gangland syndicate
which is now planning to streamline its image.
The whorehouse takes up various floors of a
skyscraper hotel, and he is received by a lovely
young receptionist in a sexy uniform, who sits
him at a teakwood interview desk and asks how
much money he wants to spend. She explains
that prices range from five dollars up to one
thousand dollars, depending on the quality and
number of girls wanted. Everything is shown on
the television intercom. The higher prices are
for the lower floors, which have higher ceilings,
mirrors over the beds, three and four girls in
bed with you at one time, etcetera. Lower
prices are for lesser delights, ending with five
dollars for a "coal-black nigger mammy with
big nostrils", as the lovely young receptionist
explains.

The client thinks it over. "Haven't you anything cheaper than five?" he asks at last.

"Of course," says the receptionist. "Seventh floor – roof garden. One dollar a shot. Self-service."

Money is certainly associated with sex, because sex can be purchased. And anything that can be purchased is part of the world of money. Remember one thing: your life will remain empty if you know only things which can be purchased, if you know only things which can be sold. Your life will remain utterly futile if your acquaintance is only with commodities. Become acquainted with things which cannot be purchased and cannot be sold – then for the first time you start growing wings, for the first time you start soaring high.

One great king, Bimbisara, reached Mahavira. He had heard that Mahavira had attained DHYANA – meditation, samadhi. In Jaina terminology it is called SAMAYIK – the ultimate state of prayer or meditation. Bimbisara had everything of this world. He became worried: "What is this samayik? What is this samadhi?" He could not rest at ease, because now for the first time he was aware that there was one thing he had not got – and he was not a man to remain contented without getting anything that took his fancy. He traveled to the mountains, found Mahavira, and said, "How much do you want for your samayik? I have come to purchase it. I can give you anything you desire, but give me this samayik, this samadhi, this meditation – what is this? Where is it? First let me look at it!"

Mahavira was surprised at the whole stupidity of the king, but he was a very polite man, soft, graceful. He said, "You need not have traveled so far. In your own capital I have a follower who has attained to the same state, and he is so poor that he may be willing to sell it. I am not willing, because I don't need any money. You can see I am naked, I don't need any clothes, I am utterly satisfied – I don't have any needs, so what will I do with your money? Even if you give me your whole kingdom I am not going to accept it. I had my own kingdom – that I have renounced. I had all that you have got!"

And Bimbisara knew it, that Mahavira had had all and had renounced, so it was difficult to persuade this man to sell. Certainly, money meant nothing to him. So he said, "Okay, who is this man? Give me his address." And Mahavira told him, "He is very poor, lives in the poorest part of your city. You may never have visited that part. This is the address... you go and ask him. He is your subject, he can sell it to you, and he is in much need. He has a wife and children and a big family and is really poor." It was a joke. Bimbisara returned happy, went directly to the poor parts of his capital where he had never been. People could not believe their eyes – his golden chariot and thousands of soldiers following him. They stopped in front of the poor man's hut. The poor man came, touched the feet of the king, and said, "What can I do? Just order me." The king said, "I have come to purchase the thing called samadhi, meditation, and I am ready to pay any price you ask." The poor man started crying, tears rolled down his cheeks, and he said, "I am sorry. I can give you my life, I can die for you right now, I can cut off my head – but how can I give you my samadhi? It is not sellable, it is not purchasable – it is not a commodity at all. It is a state of consciousness. Mahavira must have played a joke on you."

Unless you know something which cannot be sold and cannot be purchased, unless you know something which is beyond money, you have not known real life. Sex is not beyond money – love is. Transform your sex into love, and transform your love into prayer – so one day even kings like Bimbisara may feel jealous of you. Become a Mahavira, a Buddha, become a Christ, a Zarathustra, a Lao Tzu. Only then have you lived, only then have you known the mysteries of life!

Money and sex are the lowest, and people are living only in the world of money and sex – and they think they are living. They are not living, they are only vegetating, they are only dying. This is not life. Life has many more kingdoms to be revealed, an infinite treasure which is not of this world. Neither sex can give it to you, nor money. But you can attain to it. You can use your sex energy to attain it, and you can use your money power to attain it. Of course, it cannot be attained by money or by sex, but you can use your sex energy, your money power, in such an artful way that you can create a space in which the beyond can descend.

I am not against sex, and I am not against money, remember it. Always remember! But I am certainly for helping you go beyond them – I am certainly for going beyond.

Use everything as a step. Don't deny anything. If you have money, you can meditate more easily than the poor person. You can have more time to yourself. You can have a small temple in your house; you can have a garden, rose-bushes, where meditation will be easier. You can allow yourself a few holidays in the mountains, you can go into isolation and live without worry. If you have money, use it for something which money cannot purchase, but for which money can create a space.

Sexual energy is a wastage if it only remains confined to sex, but it becomes a great blessing if it starts transforming its quality: sex not for sex's sake – use sex as a communion of love. Use sex as a meeting of two souls, not only of two bodies. Use sex as a meditative dance of two persons' energies. And the dance is far richer when man and woman are dancing together –and sex is the ultimate in dance: two energies meeting, merging, dancing, rejoicing.

But use it as a stepping-stone, as a jumping-board. And when you reach the climax of your sex orgasm, become aware of what is happening, and you will be surprised – time has disappeared, mind has disappeared, ego has disappeared. For a moment there is utter silence. This silence is the real thing!

This silence can be attained through other means, too, and with less wastage of energy. This silence, this mindlessness, this timelessness, can be attained through meditation. In fact, if a person consciously goes into his sex experience, he is bound to become a meditator sooner or later. His consciousness of the sex experience is bound to make him aware that the same can happen without any sexuality involved in it. The same can happen just sitting silently by yourself, doing nothing. The mind can be dropped, time can be dropped, and the moment you drop mind and time and the ego, you are orgasmic.

The sexual orgasm is very momentary, and whatsoever is momentary brings frustration in its wake, brings misery and unhappiness and sadness and repentance. But the quality of being orgasmic can become a continuity in you, a continuum – it can become your very flavor. But it is possible only through meditation, not through sex alone.

Use sex, use money, use the body, use the world, but we have to reach God. Let God remain always the goal. Enough for today.

CHAPTER 8

I Am Not
Against Money

Beloved Osho,

What is money and why are most people deeply uncomfortable about it in one way or another?

It is a touchy question, because money is not what it appears. Money is more deep-rooted. Money is not just there outside in the currency notes, it is something to do with your inner mind and attitudes. Money is your love of things, money is your escape from persons, money is your security against death, money is your effort to control life, money is a thousand and one things. Money is not just in the currency notes otherwise things would have been very easy.

Money is your love – love of things, not of persons. The most comfortable love is of things because things are dead, you can possess them easily. You can possess a big house, a palace – the greatest palace you can possess easily – but you cannot possess even the smallest baby; even that baby rejects, even that baby fights for his freedom. A small baby, howsoever small, is dangerous for the man who wants to possess. It will rebel, it will

I AM NOT AGAINST MONEY

109

become rebellious, but it will not allow anybody to possess it.

People who cannot love persons start loving money because money is a means to possess things. The more money you have, the more things you can possess; and the more things you can possess, the more you can forget about persons. You will have many things but you will not have any contentment because deep contentment comes only when you love a person. The money will not revolt but it cannot respond also, that is the trouble. That's why miserly people become very ugly. Nobody has responded to their love ever. How can you be beautiful without love falling on you, without love showering on you like flowers – how can you be beautiful? You become ugly. You become closed. A man who possesses money or tries to possess money, is miserly and he will always be afraid of persons and people because if they are allowed to come closer they may start sharing. If you allow somebody closeness you have to allow some sharing also. People who love things become like things – dead, closed. Nothing vibrates in them, nothing dances and sings in them, their hearts have lost the beat, they live a mechanical life. They drag, burdened, burdened with many things, but they don't have any freedom because only love can give you freedom; and love can give you freedom only if you give freedom to love.

People who are afraid of love become possessive about money. People who love become non-possessive, money doesn't matter much. If it is, it is okay, it can be used; if it is not, that too is okay, because love is such a kingdom that no money can purchase it. Love is such a deep fulfillment that you can be a beggar on the street and you can sing if you have love in your heart. If you have loved and you have been loved, love crowns you, makes a king of you. Money simply makes you ugly.

I am not against money. I am not saying: "Go and throw it away," because that is another extreme. That is also the last step of the miserly mind. A man who has suffered too much because of money, who has clung to money and could not love anybody or become open, becomes so frustrated in the end that he throws away the money, renounces and goes to the Himalayas, enters a Tibetan monastery and becomes a lama. This man has not understood. If you understand, money can be used, but people who don't understand are either misers, they can't use the money, or they renounce the money, because in renouncing they are also saving the same mind. Now there will be no difficulty in using it: you renounce all and escape. But they cannot use the money, they are afraid of using it.

They can renounce, remember this. I have seen misers renouncing completely, totally. A man founded a university in Sagar in India, I was a student there. This man was a rare specimen, his name was Dr. Hari Singh Gaur. I have never come across a greater miser than him and I have not come across a greater renouncer either. He was perfect in both the ways. For his whole life he never gave a single paise to anybody, no beggar ever received anything from his bungalow.

If it was known in his town, Sagar, that some beggar was going to Hari Singh's house to ask, others would laugh and they would say: "Seems to be new to the town." Nobody ever received anything. He never donated a single rupee for any cause, humanitarian or anything. For the Indian National Freedom Movement he never donated a single paise – no, that was not his way. He was a perfect miser and he was one of the greatest lawyers in the world. He had three offices, one in India, one in China, one in England, and he worked four months in England, four months in India, four months in China. He was one of the best lawyers in the world. He accumulated so much money and then in the end he donated his whole life's savings. The whole university of Sagar is created by a single person's donation. It is one of the most beautiful universities.

But when he donated, he donated all. You will be surprised to know that he donated so absolutely that he did not leave a single paise for his children. Now they are fighting in the courts, they have nothing, they are beggars on the street. The miser remains a miser to the very end, even when he renounces. He couldn't give to his children even a single paise but he could renounce the whole.

First you can accumulate money like a madman, then one day you understand that you wasted your whole life. When you understand this you become afraid, but the old habit persists. You can give the whole and forget about it and escape, but you cannot share it.

If a man of understanding has money he shares it because money is not for itself, it is for life. If he feels that life needs it, love needs it, he can throw it away completely, but it is not a renunciation, it is again using it. Love is the goal for him; money is never the goal, money is the means. For people who are after money, money is the goal, love becomes just a means. Even their prayer is for money; even prayer becomes a means to money. Money is a very complex phenomenon. Why do people get so much into it, and so many people at that? It has a certain appeal, a magnetic appeal. Money has a hypnotic appeal in it and the appeal is that you can possess it completely. Money is very docile, it becomes a slave. The ego feels very fullfilled.

Love is not docile, love is rebellious. You cannot possess love. You can possess a woman, you can possess a man, but you can never possess love. If you possess a woman, the woman has become money, a thing; if you possess a man, the man has become money, a thing, an instrument. A man is a man and a woman is a woman only when they are an end unto themselves, not a means to anything else. Money is the means, and to become obsessed with the means is the greatest foolishness that can occur to a man and the greatest curse. Money should not become the goal, but I am not saying at the same time that you should renounce it and become beggars – use it, it is a good means. I'm not against money, I have nothing to say against it. I am saying something about you and your possessiveness, not about money. Money can be beautiful – if it is not possessed, if you don't become obsessed with it. It can be beautiful. Money is like blood circulating in the body: in the body of society money circulates, it is blood. It helps society to be enriched, to be alive – but it is like blood.

You must have heard about diseases in which the blood stops and cannot circulate, clots of blood come into existence and they become blocks and the blood cannot circulate in the body. Then you are paralyzed and if the clots happen in the heart you are dead.

If money circulates, moves from one hand to another, goes on moving, the more movement the better, then the blood circulates well, then life is healthy. But when a miser comes in, a clot has happened; somewhere somebody is accumulating, not sharing, and that is a clot in the blood circulation. The man disturbs, he does not live himself and because of his blocking he does not allow others to live. The money has stopped circulating. Blood circulating is life, blood stopped, blocked, is death. Money circulating is life, money stopped, blocked, is death.

I'm for a society where money moves fast, nobody clings to it, everybody uses it, and you remember that the simple law of money is: the more you use it, the more valuable it is. For example, we are sitting here. If ten persons have a hundred rupees in their pockets, and they keep it to themselves, then ten persons have only one thousand rupees, dead. But when those rupees circulate, if they make two rounds, ten thousand have become twenty thousand; if they make three rounds they have become thirty thousand; and if they make four rounds.... The more they circulate, the more money there is, because when one hundred rupees are kept by one man those hundred rupees are dead. If he uses them they go to somebody else, then they come to him again because others are also using them; now he has two hundred rupees, and again three hundred, four hundred, five hundred.... The more you use it, the more money floats and circulates, and the richer society is.

America is richest because America is the least miserly country in the world. Money circulates fast; everybody is using that money which he has, and even that money which he is going to have in the future, he is using it too. The country is bound to become rich. A country like India is bound to remain poor because people cling. If you cling to money the country will remain poor. When nobody uses it, money becomes like clots in blood. India has two types of people: misers and renouncers. Both these types are wrong, ill, abnormal, neurotic. One should have money, earn money, produce money – and use it. One should hold it only to use and one should use it only to hold; it becomes a circle. Then a person is both, a miser and a renouncer together. When you are miser and renouncer together you are neither miser nor renouncer, you simply enjoy whatsoever money can give. Money can give many things and money cannot give many things; when you use it then you know what money can give. Money can give all that is outward – things of this world, nothing is wrong in them. Nothing is wrong in having a beautiful house. Nothing is wrong in having a beautiful garden – money can give it to you. But money cannot give you love, that is expecting too much from poor money.

One should expect only that which can be expected, one should not move in the impossibilities. Just asking poor money to give you love – poor money cannot do it. But nothing is wrong, don't get angry with the money! Don't burn it and throw it in the river and go to the Himalayas. In the first place you asked something which a man of understanding would never have asked – you are foolish, that's all. Nothing is wrong with the money. A wandering monk came to see me two or three years ago and he was very much against money. He would not even touch it – this is a neurosis. There are people who only count money the whole day, and in the night also, in their minds, they go on counting. They touch only money with a loving hand, they never touch anybody else with a loving hand. When they look at their currency notes, watch their eyes – they sparkle. They are hypnotized. These are neurotic people. Then there are other neurotics.... This wandering monk came to me, he would not touch money. So I said: "Then it must be very difficult for you. How did you come to Bombay to see me?" He said: "There is nothing difficult." He showed two other men, his disciples: they could touch, they were not such evolved beings. What foolishness! They could purchase the ticket and they could keep the money, but for him, he said: "I don't touch, I have gone far beyond it."

I said: "But what is the point? Now you are not only using money, you are using two other persons as your pockets. You have reduced two persons, alive persons, to pockets; you have murdered. What was wrong in keeping it in your own pocket?"

And the man said: "So it seems you are in favour of money? What can money give? Can money give love? Can money give God?" I said: "You are foolish if you ask love and God from poor money, your expectations are false. Money never promised them to you, but whatsoever money promises it can give. It never promises that it can give you love. If you expect it you are idiotic." These people who have been expecting too much from money one day become enemies of money. Then they escape, then they don't touch money. Even Vinoba closes his eyes if you bring money to him, he will not see it. What nonsense! What is wrong in money? Something still seems to be miserly inside, something still seems to be like a wound, otherwise why close your eyes? What is wrong in a currency note? It is just paper, and these spiritual people go on saying that it is just paper. If you put ordinary paper in their hands, they touch it, but when you put a currency note there they throw it away as if it is a scorpion or very deadly disease. Neurosis can move from one extreme to another. Use money. Money is beautiful as far as it goes, and it goes far enough! As far as the world is concerned it goes far enough, but don't expect love, because it is of the interior, of the inner being, and don't ask for God, because it is transcendental.

Use everything for its own capacities, not for your dreams. Then you are a healthy man, and to be healthy is to be holy. Don't be abnormal in any way. Be normal, ordinary, and just create more understanding so that you can see. Money can be used, should be used, it can give you a beautiful world. Otherwise, sooner or later, if you are against money you will create a dirty country like India: everything is dirty – but they think they are great spiritualists. Everything has gone ugly but they think they are great spiritualists because they have renounced. That's why things have got so bad. They think one has to close one's eyes and not look outside. It is good to look outside because outside is God's creation; it is good to look inside because inside is sitting the Creator. Both are good. Eyes are meant to blink; they are not meant to remain open forever and they are not meant to be closed forever. They are meant to blink – open and close, open and close. That is the rhythm – out and in, out and in.

Look outside – the beautiful creation; look inside – the beautiful God. And by and by you will see that the in and out meet and mingle and are one.

CHAPTER 9

Politics:
A Blind Trip Of Ego

Beloved Osho,

Is Zen against politics?

Zen is so much against politics that it never talks about it. It is so much against politics that it cannot even be against it. If you are against it, it will affect you. Then somehow you will remain in some way related to it. To be against is to be related. When you are very much against, you are very, very related. It is a way of relationship – you are related to your enemy too, sometimes even more than you are related to your friend. Zen is so much against politics that it does not say anything about it, but it is against it. Any religion, any religion worth calling a religion, is bound to be against politics because the very phenomenon of religion is non-political.

What is politics? Politics is ambition, politics is ego, politics is aggression, politics is violence, politics is an ego-trip. How can a religious person be political? He can pretend that he is religious but he cannot be religious. And how can a political person be religious? He can pretend that he is religious but he cannot be religious. These two things cannot go together because to be religious one has to drop ambition. And if you drop ambition politics disappears. To be religious one has to drop the ego, and when you drop the ego, politics is dropped. A religious person has to be without any ego whatsoever. So religion as such is anti-political or non-political. But the religions that you see around you – Hinduism, Mohammedanism, Christianity, Jainism, Buddhism are all political. They are no longer religious. Whenever a religion becomes too organized, whenever religion becomes all establishment, whenever religion has a vested interest in the society, in this particular society, in the STATUS QUO, then it is no longer religion. A Buddha is religious, Buddhism is not religious. Jesus is religious – that's why he was crucified by the politicians – but Christians are not religious, they are very, very political.

A large political meeting was attended by a small boy trying to sell four young puppy dogs. Finally, a man approached the boy and asked jokingly, "Are these political pups, sonny?"

"Yes, sir."

"Well, then," said the man, "I'll take these two."

A week later at the same place there was a religious gathering and the same boy showed up to sell the remaining two dogs. A man walked up to him and asked, "My little lad, what kind of puppies are these you have?"

"These are religious pups, sir."

The first man who purchased the other two dogs happened to overhear this.

"Say," he said, "didn't you tell me that those pups that I bought from you last week were political pups?"

"Yes, sir," said the young dog-seller, "but these puppies aren't – they've got their eyes open."

Politics is blind. It is a blind trip of the ego. One goes on groping to find some source of power so that one can feel, "I am somebody." Politics comes out of an inferiority complex. Deep down you feel that you are nobody, deep down you are afraid of your nothingness. You cannot accept it. You have to deny it. Politics is a denial of your inner nothingness, religion is rejoicing in it.

Let me repeat it. Politics is an effort to deny your inner nothingness. Of course, you can never succeed in it because that inner nothingness is your very nature, it cannot be denied. Your interpretation is wrong. That inner nothingness has nothing to do with inferiority complex, it is your interpretation that creates the inferiority complex. And out of the inferiority complex you start to become superior – you become a prime minister, you become a president or something. This inner nothingness drives you somewhere – it may be to money, it may be to power, it may be prestige, it may be knowledge, it may even be to renunciation – but this inner nothingness drives you to find some way to forget that you are nothing, to start feeling that you are somebody, that you are something important, valuable, significant, that without you the world will be at a loss.

This inner nothingness is a driving force towards politics, but nobody can succeed in denying it. You can manage to postpone it but again and again it will assert itself, again and again it will be there sitting on the throne, again and again when you think you have arrived you will know, deep down, whenever you look inside, that you have not arrived. The inner nothingness is untouched by whatsoever you have done, by whatsoever you have accumulated, by whatsoever you have achieved – it remains untouched, that emptiness is still there. That's the misery of the successful man. Nothing fails like success. Failure is never such a failure as success is a failure because the person who has failed can still hope. In failure the hope that you may succeed some day is still there, but in success all hope disappears.

I have heard about President Coolidge, one of the great American Presidents. When his term was over he declined to stand again for the presidency although there was every possibility that he would be chosen again. He was very much loved – he was such a silent man. So people started approaching him and asking,

"Why? Why are you not standing again? It is almost certain you will be chosen." But he would say no. And he would say no with very deep, sad eyes. Finally somebody forced him to answer exactly why he went on saying no. He said, "Because I have come to know that there is nothing in it and to repeat it a second time will be stupid. I have come to know that nothing is gained by gaining such things. I remain the same person."

How can a chair change you? You can sit on a golden chair or you can sit on a very, very ordinary stool, it doesn't make any difference – you remain the same. How can the chair change you? How can the change of the chair change you? But this is how the politician goes on befooling himself. No. A religious person cannot be a politician. A religious person, by his very religiousness, is non-political. He approaches life in a totally different way. What is the difference? What is the radical difference? The radical difference is that the religious man does not interpret his nothingness as inferiority. That is the revolution. The day it happens that your inner nothingness is not inferiority, that your nothingness is your very being.... It is the way God is in you. God's way of being present is being absent – that's how God is present in the world. He is so non-violent that he remains absent.

Deep inside you the hole that you feel, the dark hole, is not dark. It is luminous with light. Enter into it. And it is not nothing, it is the very secret of the whole

POLITICS: A BLIND TRIP OF EGO

life, the whole existence. It is all. That nothingness is just the way God appears to those people who don't look deeply. It is a misunderstanding. The religious man befriends his nothingness. That's what meditation is all about: befriending your nothingness. He enjoys it. He celebrates it. He dances it. He sings it. He goes again and again into it. Whenever he has a chance, whenever he has the opportunity, he closes his eyes, he drops into his nothingness, he disappears there. This is the very door of God. From there you connect yourself to the divine. Once you have started enjoying your nothingness, who bothers about politics?

Nixon was out walking along the beach at San Clemente and decided to go for a swim. He got out beyond the waves and suddenly began drowning. Three teenage boys happened to come along, dived into the ocean, and pulled Nixon ashore. When he had regained his breath, Nixon thanked the boys. "In appreciation," he said, "I'd be willing to use my influence to help you boys in any way I could. Is there anything special you want? "I'd like to go to West Point!" said one boy.

"I believe I can arrange that," said the ex-President.

"I'd like to go to Annapolis!" said another boy.

"I'll see to it immediately," said Nixon.

."I'd like to be buried in Arlington Cemetery," announced the third boy.

"That's a very strange request," said Mr. Nixon. "Why would you want to be buried in Arlington Cemetery?"

"Well," said the youngster, "my father is a religious man and when I get home and tell him who I saved from drowning, he's gonna kill me!"

Remember, the politician is always there. Till the ego is completely thrown away it is always there. The ego is the politician. If you are egoistic, you are political. You may not stand in an election, you may not strive for any political power, but if you have the ego you will remain political in subtle ways. You may dominate your wife or your husband, you may dominate your children, you may dominate your servants. You will remain cunning and you will never miss any opportunity to dominate.

So when I use the word "political" I don't just mean state affairs, no, I mean all affairs where domination is involved. If you want to have more money you are political because if you want to have more money you will have to exploit people. If you want to have more power you will have to fight. If you want more prestige you will have to be competitive. Your so-called saints are all political. They have their ambitions. Each saint wants to become the greatest saint — then he is political, then he will have to fight with other saints who are competitors.

A religious person is non-competitive and that's why I insist again and again – I am never tired of this insistence – on you being meditative, because meditation is the only joy which is non-competitive, the only joy that you attain but nobody loses because you attain. Nobody is a loser. If you have more money somebody will have less money; if you have more power somebody will have less power; if Morarji becomes the prime minister, Indira is no longer a Prime Minister. Somebody loses. Somebody's gain is going to be somebody else's loss.

But a religious person will not like to do anything in which somebody becomes a loser. This is violent, this is ugly, this is inhuman. Then what is left for the religious person? He can celebrate his being. He can meditate. In meditation you gain and nobody loses. Only God is infinite, everything else is finite. Money is finite, power is finite… if you have it somebody will not have it. Only God is infinite. You can have as much as you like. You can have the whole of it and yet nobody is a loser. That's the beauty of religion – it is non-violent joy, it is non-competitive joy.

A panhandler stopped a Congressman on a Washington street and asked him for a dime.

"A dime won't buy anything these days," said the politician. "Don't you want a quarter?"

"No," replied the panhandler, "with all the shady politicians around here I'm afraid to carry too much cash."

He is right.

And this is one from the twentieth century, somewhere in the twentieth century.... The anchorman on an educational TV late night news programme surprised his viewers with this announcement:

"We have good news and bad news for you. First the bad news: our planet is being invaded by Martians. And now for the good news: they eat politicians and pee gasoline."

Ichazo reckons that our culture, the whole society, is now raising its consciousness, that we are no longer on an individual trip but that humanity is beginning to awaken. And he says that the utopian vision of humanity as one enormous Jamily is now a practical necessity.

This is how politics enters into religion. And this is nothing new. Down the ages there have been people saying it again and again. This is how fascism enters into religion. This is what Friedrich Nietzsche was saying and he became the originator of Adolf Hitler and his philosophy. He was saying that now humanity had come to a point where it was going to enter into a new arena, the arena of super-humanity, superhumans. This is what Sri Aurobindo was saying in India – he was basically a politician and he remained a politician to the very end. He was also saying that now we had come to a point where collective effort, not individual effort, was needed.

Remember that these ideas about collective effort are dangerous. That's how politics enters into religion. Religion is utterly individual and will remain individual. Only the individual can meditate. When you meditate you disappear from the collective world. If you start meditating here with five hundred people you may start with five hundred people but the moment you enter into meditation you are alone. Those four hundred and ninety-nine are no more. Meditation is a movement in tremendous aloneness. It has nothing to do with the collective. You can meditate together but when you go into meditation you go alone.

Three words will have to be understood: the collective, the individual and the universal. Ichazo goes on getting confused between the universal and the collective. The individual is in the middle, the collective is below the individual, and the universal is above the individual. If the individual becomes part of collectivity, he loses something, he is no longer as conscious as he was before, he is no longer alert. That's why in a crowd you are no longer as responsible as you were when you were alone. A crowd can commit great sins. In a crowd you don't feel responsibility. The collective is lower than the individual – all the great sins of history can be attributed to the collective. The individual is far better than the collective.

You see a mob burning a Hindu temple or a Mohammedan mosque. If you get each individual from the mob and enquire, he will say, "I did not really want to do it but other people were doing it and I was just standing there so I got into it." No individual Mohammedan will be able to say with a clear heart that he has done a great thing, a great job, a religious thing, in burning a Hindu temple. And no Hindu will say that he has done a great thing by killing a Mohammedan or by burning a mosque. But he will say that in the crowd he was lost. You may have also felt it. In a crowd you become lower than you ordinarily are. In a crowd you become baser, you become lower; you are more animal than you are human. The collective is animal, the individual is human and the universal is divine. When a person enters into meditation, he does not become a part of the collective, he becomes dissolved into the universal which is a higher point than the individual itself.

But politicians always talk about the collective. They are always interested in changing the society – because in changing the society, in making efforts to change the society and the structure of society and this and that, they become powerful. The society has never been changed. It remains the same – the same rotten thing. And it will remain the same unless it is understood that all consciousness happens in the individual. And when it happens, the individual becomes universal. If it happens to many individuals then the society is changed – but not as a social thing, not collectively.

Let me explain it to you. There are five hundred people here. You cannot be changed as a collective unit, there is no way. You cannot be made divine as a collective unit, there is no way. Your souls are individual, your consciousnesses are individual.

But if out of these five hundred people, three hundred people become transformed, then the whole collective will have a new quality. But these three hundred people will go through individual changes, through individual mutations. Then the collective will have a higher consciousness because these three hundred people are pouring their consciousness into the collective, they are there. When one man becomes a Buddha, the whole existence becomes a little more awakened – just by his presence. Even if he is a drop in the ocean then too the ocean, at least as far as one drop is concerned, is more alert, more aware. When that drop disappears into the ocean it raises the quality of the ocean. Each individual being transformed changes the society. When many, many individuals are changed, the society changes. That is the only way to change it, not the other way round. You cannot change the society. If you want to change the society directly your effort is political. Ichazo must be getting political. It happens. When you start becoming powerful religiously, when you start leading many people, when you become a leader, then great ideas start happening in the mind. Then the mind says that now the whole humanity can be changed, now we should plan for a great change of the whole humanity. Then greed grows, ambition grows, ego expects. This has always happened and this will happen always. Beware of it.

Never become a victim of the idea of the collective; the collective is lower than you. You have to become universal. The universal is not social, the universal is existential. You have to fall in tune with the whole existence, you have to get hooked with the dance of the universe – not with the social, not with small communities or sects, not with Christians and Hindus and Mohammedans, not with this earth, not with the East, not with the West, not with this century. You have to get hooked with the whole of it, the whole existence.

But that is higher than the individual. The mass is a pitfall. The mob is always there to pull you down. And it happens to so-called religious people. Ichazo is not really very religious to me. He has gathered techniques from here and there, he is very eclectic. From Gurdjieff's work, from Sufis, he has gathered a few techniques. He is a technician. He knows the technology but he does not know the goal. And he himself has not attained to it. But he is very, very technically expert, skillful. His movement, Arica, can turn into a fascist's movement any day. It creates a kind of fascism in its followers.

There are a few Aricans here – ex-Aricans, I should say. The ways of the Aricans are very political. Just a few months ago, Amida – Amida was very close to Ichazo for many years – received a letter saying that she was expelled. Expulsion is basically political. How can you expel? What do you mean by expulsion? This is monopoly. She has come to me so she is expelled from Arica. Now my books and my tapes are not allowed there. No Arican is allowed to read my books. This is political. What nonsense! This is monopoly, possessiveness. This is how politics comes into being. A religious mind is an open mind. You have to see, you have to listen to everybody, you have to learn from everybody. You should not be closed. Being with a really enlightened Master you become very, very open to existence, utterly open. You will even be open to the Devil if he comes to teach you something. You will be open and you will learn and you will trust yourself. There is no fear because you know yourself – he cannot deceive you. These people who become so afraid that somebody may get out of the fold, may get hooked with somebody else, are really basically doubting their own philosophy. They don't believe in their own philosophy. They know that somewhere something may be better, somewhere somebody may be higher, and people will go there and they will leave them. Their fear is the fear of losing followers, so they create China Walls around them.

No, it never happens when there is a religious person. He gives you his love, he gives you his being, he gives you his wisdom, and he makes you free. And you can go on and on learning and each learning will prove that your Master is right. That is the trust. Wherever you go, even if you go to somebody who is against me and you listen to him, if I am right, listening to him will prove that I am right. It will not be a loss, you will become richer.

Trust needs no fear, love needs no fear. But it is not love, it is not trust, it is just fear – a fear is being created. If you go somewhere else you will be expelled. And people are very afraid of things like expulsion. Is this a communist party or what? Expulsion? People are very much afraid of being expelled because they want to belong to some group because they don't have any soul of their own. In the group they feel good, they belong to a certain community – the chosen few, the elite, the heralds of a new world which is going to come, the leaders of the new world, the supermen, the first race of the super-men. They feel very good.

But that you feel only in the group; when you are alone you become suspicious. And when you are in the group you need not feel responsibility. The group takes it from you, you are relaxed, the group takes care. You have been brought up in dependence. First you were dependent on your parents. Then you become dependent on your own family – the wife, the husband – then you become dependent on your children, on the society, the state, the church, the family, the community. You have always lived a life of dependence.

So when you go to a Master you again want somebody to depend on. But a real Master will not help you to depend on him, a real Master will try to make you independent. His whole effort will be that you should become your own being. That's what Zen people do.

I was reading just the other day...

A young man came to Hui Neng again and again. Hui Neng was very rough. Only Zen Masters can be rought. Why? Because if they really want you to be independent they are rough. He was very rough. He would slap the young man, he would close the door in his face, he would shout – and once he threw him out of the window and he fell about fifteen feet into a ditch. And not only that – then Hui Neng looked out of the window and laughed. Certainly the man left him. This was the last straw. Enough is enough. He left him immediately, he didn't come back for one year. And he went to other Masters and he learned many things and he roamed about and then one day, sitting silently in a cave, he became enlightened – the first *satori* happened. And then you know what? He rushed back to Hui Neng to thank him. The day that the *satori* happened he knew that exactly the same situation had been created when he had been thrown into the ditch. He had missed. But now he knew because now he had again come to that point, he had come to that situation inside. Just a moment before the *satori* happened he was surprised to see that this was the same situation inside as Hui Neng had managed to create when he had thrown him out of the window and when he had looked down and he had laughed. And he had missed! That man had tremendous compassion.

He came rushing towards Hui Neng. He touched his feet and he said, "Master, thank you. Thank you that you were so rough with me. Thank you that you never taught me except to beat me. Thank you for all that you have done for me."

A real Master wants a disciple to become a Master in his own right. But ordinarily you don't want that independence yourself, you want somebody to cling to. You are a clinger. You want somebody to be very authoritative, somebody to sit on a high throne and say to you, "You don't worry, I will take care of you. You forget all about everything. I am here so I will take care. You simply come and follow me." But if somebody is like that remember that this is a sure sign – this authoritativeness, this taking other people's responsibility – this is a sure sign that the man himself wants people to depend on him. He is dependent on his dependents. He enjoys it. He loves the idea that so many people are dependent on him. He himself is dependent, remember; he is not different from you. It is the same trip from the other end. If you all leave him he will suffer as much as you will suffer. Sometimes he may suffer more because his investment is more. If you leave a man like Ichazo, if all his followers disappear, he may go mad or he may commit suicide. He will be very shaky, he will tremble, he will not know what has happened, he will lose all his self-confidence. He gains all his self-confidence when he looks into your eyes and sees that you are looking towards him and you feel that he is right, he is true, he is the Master. When he sees that look in your eyes, when he sees that reflection in your eyes he feels confident. Yes. It is so. This is a mutual deception. My approach is absolutely non-political, hence it is absolutely individual. And that is the religious approach as such. Religion will remain individual, it will never become a collective phenomenon, it cannot. Politics will always become collective, it will never become individual.

Politics is collective, religion is individual, spirituality is universal. Remember it.

CHAPTER 10

Leave The
Politicians Aside

Beloved Osho,

On one hand the world is preparing for a global suicide; it looks like there is not much time left for our growth. On the other hand, what I heard from you is that growth is only possible when we relax, sit silently and wait. This is a paradox. Beloved Osho, please can you speak about how to come out of situations where one part of me is restless and wants to do something?– Yet deep down I feel that this leads me nowhere.

It is not a paradox, it only appears so. The world is certainly preparing for a global suicide; about that there are not two opinions – it is becoming every day more and more certain. Naturally you think you have to do something to prevent it. It is beyond your doing; whatever you do will bring it closer.

What can you do? The power is not in your hands; the power is in hands which are absolutely stubborn, and they don't care a bit what happens to humanity. Their ego is their supreme value, the only value. Even though it means their own destruction, they will take the risk; they will destroy whoever they think is their enemy.

In the beginning, when this kind of war material was in the hands of two countries, the Soviet Union and America, there was some possibility that they may come to some negotiation. Now with the power of nuclear weapons in five countries, the possibility of negotiation has become more difficult, more complicated. And by the end of this century, the power will be in twenty-five countries' hands. Then the question of negotiation does not arise. My suggestion is: time is certainly very short, but it is enough to become enlightened, and it is enough to spread an enlightened atmosphere around the world. That is the only possibility.

If we can make the people of the world... not the politicians, leave them aside; they have the power but without the consent of the people of the world, their power is not of much use. If armies simply say, "No, we are not going to use nuclear weapons," if the scientists simply say, "No, we are not going to produce any more nuclear weapons," if the whole intelligentsia of the world unanimously creates a great uproar: "It is not a question of war; wars we have seen in thousands – they have been destructive, but they have not destroyed all life. This is not war, this is simple suicide!"

But these people: the scientists, the armies, the intelligentsia, the poets, the musicians, the mystics, the painters, the actors – the people who have a certain impact on the masses, although they don't have any power except their individuality and their creativity – if they join hands together, this global suicide can be avoided. Not only suicide can be avoided, but with the same energy that was going to destroy all life, the planet can be turned into a paradise.

Energy is neutral – it can destroy, it can create. Nobody has thought: What can be the creative use of atomic energy? What can be the creative use of nuclear weapons? If the destructive power is so great, the power for creation will be equally great. Hence, I say not only can global suicide be avoided, but we can bring into existence a new dawn, a new man, a new humanity.

Perhaps for the first time there can be an authentic civilization which loves peace, which is compassionate, which is creative, which drops all discriminations of nations, religions, races, and makes this whole globe one family.

Once there are no discriminations of religions, races, nations, war becomes impossible.

We have to avoid the suicide that is oncoming and we have to change the whole structure of the world so that war itself becomes impossible. All our efforts, all our energies... seventy-five percent of human energy is pouring into creating war material. We are living only on twenty-five percent of our energy. If that seventy-five percent is also released for living, there will be no poverty, there will be no sickness. Life can be prolonged. People can live young until their last breath; they need not become old.

All this is possible, and for this, there is enough time. But you have to understand perfectly well: anything on your part as a protest is not going to help. You will be simply crushed, ignored.... Pacifists have existed for centuries; they have not been able to avoid any war.

In fact I have seen so many processions of protest and I have always wondered... the people who were protesting were all violent: their slogans were violent, their gestures were violent. If they had power in their hands, they would start killing those people whom they think are warmongers. They are doing the same thing, they are not peaceful people; they may be pacifist in ideology, but they don't know what peace is. I want my people to know the peace, to know the silence, to know the beauty of their inner being, the blissfulness and love and light, and spread it. And spreading it is not going to be a missionary thing – you are not to convert anybody. Just your very presence, just your loving eyes, your peaceful existence – the charisma that arises with enlightenment, a certain different wavelength that the enlightened man starts radiating around him, changes people's hearts without their knowing. It is not a question of convincing them intellectually; for that, time is certainly very short. We have not been convinced for centuries, intellectually, although great efforts have been made that there should be no war, there should be no government, there should be no nations. Great intellectuals have been trying – like Bakunin, Bokharin, Leo Tolstoy, Bertrand Russell – but it has not created any visible effect anywhere. My understanding is that these people themselves were not peaceful people. They have not known anything of the eternal joy of their own interiority, the dance of their own being. They have not tasted from the springs of nectar that are at their very center. Once you have tasted your own immortality, you start spreading an invisible fire ... no intellectual argument, but people will be immensely touched by your very presence, by your aroma, by your fragrance, by your love.

We need in the world more love to balance war.

We need in the world more creativity to balance the destructive forces. We need in the world more enlightened people to balance the blind politicians. For this there is still time enough, because enlightenment can happen within a second. It does not need time; it needs only a total longing for it, a longing as if your life is at risk.

Kavina, I can understand why you are feeling a paradox. You would like to do something, but things have gone beyond your doing. What can you do to prevent the Soviet Union or to prevent Ronald Reagan? And soon nuclear weapons will be in twenty-five countries, with pygmy politicians. What can you do?

The only thing possible is: forget doing.

Think of being.

You can be more joyful, you can be more loving – that is within your capacity. No Ronald Reagan can prevent you. No nuclear weapons can prevent you. People have never thought this way. They have always tried to protest against wars – nobody has listened to them.

I am suggesting a totally new solution. And in the circumstances, that is the only alternative possible: forget doing, grow into your being. And the growth of your being is contagious; it will help many people to light their unlit torches from your life fire.

If we have people around the world who know the beauty of life, of creativity, of poetry, of music, of painting, of dancing, of love, then nobody – no politician – will have the guts to force humanity into a war. So rather than going against war, you create the balancing force – which is in your hands. If the warmongers have nuclear weapons, then you have to create something equivalent, or more powerful – and enlightenment is certainly more powerful than any nuclear weapon.

In the Old Testament, there is a beautiful story of two cities, Sodom and Gomorrah. God became very angry with these two cities, because in both people were practicing perverted sex. In Sodom people were making love to animals; hence 'sodomy' has become the word for making love with animals. In Gomorrah people had become homosexuals, and all kinds of perversions.... God finally decided to destroy both those cities completely, and in the Old Testament he did destroy Sodom and Gomorrah.

It may not be the right image of God, but the Jewish God is an angry God. That is our projection: it is not a question of whether God is angry or not. God is a hypothesis – you can make anything out of it, whatever you want. God declares in the Jewish scriptures, "I am a very angry God, very jealous. I will never forgive you if you go against me; I am not your uncle, I am not a nice man."

But in Judaism there is a rebellious stream, a very small minority stream of Hassidic mystics. The orthodox Jews don't accept them as religious at all, but as I understand it, they are the only religious people in the whole Judaic tradition. They are people who dance, sing, love, play music. They are very joyous people and they have interpreted Judaism according to their own joy and blissfulness.

They cannot tolerate such a thing, that God destroyed... and a God who is omnipotent, all powerful, he could have changed them – if he can create the whole world, can't he change two cities and their sexual perversions? Has he to resort to destruction and death? He is the father of those two cities also, and when he has all the powers... this whole universe was created by him and he could not manage to change those two cities? Hassids have changed that story and I love it, although that change is not in the Jewish scriptures. Jews will never accept that change, but I, for one, accept it. It makes a tremendous impact on anyone who can understand. The Jewish story is: When God decided to destroy Sodom and Gomorrah, a Hassidic mystic went to him and asked, "Have you decided?" God said, "I am absolutely certain; I am going to destroy these people completely." The Hassidic mystic said, "But I have a question to ask: If there are two hundred people, one hundred in each city, who are good people, who are authentically religious, who are awakened, will you still destroy those two cities? Those two hundred people will be destroyed with them. It seems you are taking too much care about the perverted and you are not taking any interest in the awakened."

God had to think it over; the argument was significant. How can he destroy the awakened people, the spiritual people, the good people? He said, "If you can prove that there are two hundred people in those cities who are awakened, enlightened, then I will not destroy them. How can I destroy them?" The Hassid – they are very beautiful people with a great sense of humor – the Hassid mystic said, "If I cannot prove two hundred but only twenty, are you going to destroy the twenty enlightened people in those two cities? Do numbers matter so much? Are you thinking of quality or of quantity?" God was at a loss to argue with this man. He said, "Okay, you prove twenty." the Hassid said, "And if I can prove only two?"

Now God was perfectly aware that the question of quality and quantity... it does not matter whether there are two enlightened people or two hundred enlightened people, they cannot be destroyed. To destroy them is to destroy the whole base, the whole foundation of religion. God said, "Okay, okay, you prove two persons!"

The Hassid said, "In fact there is only one – but he lives six months in one city and six months in the other city. What do you think about it?" From two hundred he has come down to one.

God said, "I have understood your logic. You bring that man before me." He said, "I am that man. Can't you see me? Can't you look inside me? Are you going to destroy me? – because I live six months in Sodom and six months in Gomorrah." And God had to concede: "In that case I will not destroy Sodom and Gomorrah."

Jews will not be ready to accept it, because it is not in their scriptures, but it is in the Hassidic teachings. I have loved the story, because the Hassidic mystic has proved far more intelligent than the so-called God, far more loving and compassionate than the so-called God.

Even God cannot save the world from the hands of politicians. Now you will need mystics; only mystics can create the atmosphere around the world of love and peace, of silence and joy, of song and dance; they will make life so rich that it becomes impossible for people even to think of war. Politicians will be left alone without any support from their armies, from their scientists, from their intelligentsia, from mystics, from poets. And against all this intelligence, all their nuclear weapons will become impotent. They can create war only if unconsciously we are ready to commit suicide, if in some way we are supportive to them. It is our support that has given them power. If we withdraw our support, their power disappears. They don't have any power of their own.

What power does Richard Nixon have now? Once he is no longer the president, nobody even bothers whether he is alive or dead, what he is doing; otherwise if he had just a little cold it was headline news. Now if he wants his name to be in the newspapers again, the only way is to commit suicide. But he will not be able to see it; others will read it – and that too in a small corner on the third page of the papers. Who cares about people who are no longer presidents, no longer prime ministers? It is our support that gives them power.

There is time enough to withdraw our support; there is time enough to create a non-political humanity. And the times are such that it is possible. In ordinary times you cannot convince people to withdraw their cooperation from the politicians, but the times are

can create the atmosphere around the world of love and peace, of silence and joy, of song and dance; they will make life so rich that it becomes impossible for people even to think of war. Politicians will be left alone without any support from their armies, from their scientists, from their intelligentsia, from mystics, from poets. And against all this intelligence, all their nuclear weapons will become impotent. They can create war only if unconsciously we are ready to commit suicide, if in some way we are supportive to them. It is our support that has given them power. If we withdraw our support, their power disappears. They don't have any power of their own.

What power does Richard Nixon have now? Once he is no longer the president, nobody even bothers whether he is alive or dead, what he is doing; otherwise if he had just a little cold it was headline news. Now if he wants his name to be in the newspapers again, the only way is to commit suicide. But he will not be able to see it; others will read it – and that too in a small corner on the third page of the papers. Who cares about people who are no longer presidents, no longer prime ministers? It is our support that gives them power.

There is time enough to withdraw our support; there is time enough to create a non-political humanity. And the times are such that it is possible. In ordinary times you cannot convince people to withdraw their cooperation from the politicians, but the times are abnormal and every day the war keeps coming closer. In this moment, people can choose very easily not to cooperate, because cooperation simply means committing suicide. So one thing: make people's lives more joyous so that even the unconscious desire for suicide disappears from their being. And second, make them aware the power is in your hands, and if the war happens and life disappears from the earth, you will be responsible, not the politicians. They are simply puppets. We give them power and then the puppets start behaving like masters. Withdraw the power and you will see that their size goes on becoming smaller and smaller and smaller, and they will disappear. They don't have any power of their own; it is your power given to them. Kavina, for that there is enough time. And it is a great challenge, a very adventurous time. When the world is facing suicide, the possibility is that the world can be convinced – not intellectually but through your growing hearts, your love – to let the old world die and a new world with new values be born.

You won't have such an opportunity again. In the past there was never such an opportunity. It is not to be missed. It is so simple a matter, but you have to begin with yourself. It is not that you have to do something. I am saying you have to be something: a force, a charisma, a magnet, which can pull people's hearts towards you; a poetry, a song, such that people unknowingly start being influenced by it; a dance, so that people who had forgotten how to dance suddenly feel energy arising in their feet. They would like to join you in the dance. So we are not to be against the politicians or against their nuclear weapons; we have to create a balancing force – more powerful. And once people have tasted life, which they have forgotten completely, they will automatically withdraw their support. It has already started happening. In the Vietnam war, thirty percent of the soldiers did not use their weapons. The American government was at a loss about what to do. The generals could not figure it out because such a thing had never happened – a soldier goes to war to kill. But in Vietnam it was so clear: America is doing something simply absurd – destroying poor people who have not done anything against America. And because it was the younger generation who had gone as soldiers, they could see the futility of it. Why should they be killed? Poor people working in their fields or in their orchards, small children, women – why should they be killed? They are not fighting; they are not a danger to America.

Thirty percent of the soldiers would go to the warfront every day with their guns loaded and would come back in the evening without having used their guns at all. These thirty percent have shown the way. If it can happen to thirty percent, why can't it happen to a hundred percent? – and the Vietnam war was not going to destroy all life.

Soldiers should be made aware... in fact, the whole atmosphere around the world will become a warning for everybody that politicians have gone mad and now they don't need anybody's support. Just think of it: if armies simply march and meet the enemy armies and have a beautiful dance together, and come home happily, what can the politicians do? They could have court-martialed one soldier, but they cannot court-martial all the soldiers. And who is going to court-martial them? – because the generals will be part of the dance.

A great adventurous moment is coming close to us; there is nothing to be feared. You cannot do anything to prevent it, but you can be in such a way that your very being becomes a prevention.

CHAPTER 11

Authenticity:
Real Richness,
Real Power

Beloved Osho,
It seems to me that human beings feel that just to be themselves is not enough. Why do most people have such a compulsion to reach power and prestige and so on, rather than just being simple human beings?

It is a complicated question. It has two sides, and both have to be understood.

First: you have never been accepted by your parents, teachers, neighbors, society, as you are. Everybody was trying to improve upon you, to make you better. Everybody was pointing at the flaws, at the mistakes, at the errors, at the weaknesses, at the frailties, which every human being is prone to. Nobody emphasized your beauty, nobody emphasized your intelligence, nobody emphasized your grandeur.

Just being alive is such a gift, but nobody ever told you to be thankful to existence. On the contrary, everyone was grumpy, complaining. Naturally, if everything surrounding your life from the very beginning goes on pointing out to you that you are not what you should be, goes on giving you great ideals that you have to follow and you have to become, your *is*ness is never praised. What is praised is your future – if you can become someone respectable, powerful, rich, intellectual, in some way famous, not just a nobody.

Constant conditioning against you has created in you the idea, "I am not enough as I am, something is missing. And I have to be somewhere else – not here. This is not the place I am supposed to be, but somewhere higher, more powerful, more dominant, more respected, more well known." This is half the story – which is ugly, which should not be the case. This can be simply removed if people are a little bit more intelligent about how to be mothers, how to be fathers, how to be teachers.

You are not to spoil the child. His self-respect, his acceptance of himself, you have to help it to grow. On the contrary, you are becoming a hindrance for growth. This is the ugly part but it is the simple part. It can be removed, because it is so simple and logical to see that you are not responsible for what you are, that this is the way nature has made you. Unnecessarily weeping over the spilled milk is sheer stupidity. But the second part is tremendously important. Even if all these conditioning are removed – you are deprogrammed, all these ideas are taken out of your mind – then you will still feel you are not enough; but that will be a totally different experience. The words will be the same, but the experience will be different.

You are not enough because you can be more. It will not be any longer a question of becoming famous, respectable, powerful, rich. That will not be at all your concern. Your concern will be that your being is only a seed. With birth you are not born as a tree, you are born only as a seed, and you have to grow to the point where you come to flowering, and that flowering will be your contentment, fulfillment. This flowering has nothing to do with power, nothing to do with money, nothing to do with politics. It has something to do absolutely with you; it is an individual progress. And for this, the other conditioning is a hindrance, it is a distraction, it is a misuse of a natural longing for growth.

Every child is born to grow and to become a fully-fledged human being, with love, with compassion, with silence. He has to become a celebration unto himself. It is not a question of competition, not even a question of comparison.

But the first ugly conditioning distracts you because the urge to grow, the urge to become more, the urge to expand, is being used by the society, by the vested interests. They divert it. They fill your mind so you think that this urge is to have more money, this urge means to be at the top in every way – in education, in politics. Wherever you are, you have to be at the top; less than that and you will feel you are not doing well, you will feel a deep inferiority complex.

This whole conditioning produces an inferiority complex because it wants you to become superior, more superior than others. It teaches you competition, comparison; it teaches you violence, fight. It teaches you that means don't matter, what matters is the end – success is the goal. And this can be easily done because you already are born with an urge to grow, with an urge to be somewhere else.

A seed has to travel far to become flowers. It is a pilgrimage. The urge is beautiful. It is given by nature itself. But the society, up to now, has been very cunning; it turns, deviates, diverts your natural instincts into some social utility

These two are the sides that are giving you the feeling that wherever you are, something is missing; you have to gain something, achieve something, become an achiever, a climber.

Your intelligence is needed to make it clear what your natural urge is, and what is social conditioning. Cut the social conditioning – it is all crap – so that nature remains pure, unpolluted. And nature is always individualistic.

You will grow and you will come to blossom, and you may have roseflowers. Somebody else may grow and will have marigolds. You are not superior because you have roseflowers; he is not inferior because he has marigolds. You both have come to flowering, that is the point; and that flowering gives a deep contentment. All frustration, all tension disappears; a profound peace prevails over you, the peace that passes understanding. But first you have to cut the social crap completely; otherwise it will go on distracting you.

You have to be rich but not wealthy. Richness is something else. A beggar can be rich, and an emperor can be poor. Richness is a quality of being. Alexander the Great met Diogenes, who was a naked beggar, with only a lamp – that was his only possession. And he kept his lamp lit even in the day. He was obviously behaving in a strange way; even Alexander had to ask him, "Why are you keeping this lamp lit in the day?" He raised his lamp and looked at Alexander's face, and he said, "I am looking for the real man day and night, and I don't find him." Alexander was shocked that a naked beggar should say such a thing to him, the world conqueror. But he could see that Diogenes was so beautiful in his nudity. His eyes were so silent, his face was so peaceful, his words had such an authority, his presence was so cool and calm and soothing, that although Alexander felt insulted, he could not retaliate. The presence of the man was so much, that Alexander himself looked a beggar beside him. In his diary he has written. "For the first time I felt that richness is something other than having money. I have seen a rich man."

Richness is your authenticity, sincerity, your truth, your love, your creativity, your sensitivity, your meditativeness. This is your real wealth. Society has moved your head towards mundane things, and you have forgotten completely that your head has been moved.

Your head, your mind, has been turned in many ways by many people according to their ideas of how you should be. There was not any bad intention. Your parents loved you, your teachers loved you, your society wants you to be somebody. Their intentions were good, but their understanding was very short. They forgot that you cannot manage to make a marigold bush into roseflowers, or vice-versa.

All that you can do is help the roses to grow bigger, more colorful, more fragrant. You can give all the chemicals that are needed to transform the color and the fragrance – the manure that is needed, the right soil, the right watering at the right times – but you cannot make the rose bush produce lotuses.

And if you start giving the idea to the rosebush, "You have to become lotus flowers" – and of course the lotus flowers are beautiful and big – you are giving a wrong conditioning which will help only in that this bush will never be able to produce lotuses; and also, its whole energy will be directed on a wrong path so it will not produce even roses, because from where will it get the energy to produce roses? And when there will be no lotuses, no roses, of course this poor bush will feel continuously empty, frustrated, barren, unworthy.

And this is what is happening to human beings. With all good intentions, people are turning your mind. In a better society, with more understanding people, nobody will change you. Everybody will help you to be yourself – and to be oneself is the richest thing in the world. To be oneself gives you all that you need to feel fulfilled, all that can make your life meaningful, significant. Just being yourself and growing according to your nature will bring the fulfillment of your destiny.

So the urge is not bad, but it has been moved towards wrong objects. And you have to be aware not to be manipulated by anybody, howsoever good their intentions are. You have to save yourself from so many well-intentioned people, do-gooders, who are constantly advising you to be this, to be that. Listen to them and thank them, they don't mean any harm, but harm is what happens.

You just listen to your own heart – that is your only teacher. In the real journey of life, your own intuition is your only teacher. Have you looked at the word 'intuition'? It is the same as "tuition". Tuition is given by teachers, from outside; intuition is given by your own nature, from inside. You have your guide within you. With just a little courage you will never feel that you are unworthy. You may not become the president of a country, you may not become a prime minister, you may not become Henry Ford; but there is no need. You may become a beautiful singer, you may become a beautiful painter. And it does not matter what you do.... You may become a great shoemaker.

When Abraham Lincoln became the president of America.... His father had been a shoemaker, and the whole senate was feeling a little embarrassed that a shoemaker's son should preside over the richest people, the high-class people, who believe they are superior because they have more money, because they belong to a long-standing famous family. The whole senate was in a way embarrassed, angry, irritated; nobody was happy that Lincoln had become the president.

One man, who was very arrogant, bourgeois, stood up before Lincoln gave his first, his maiden address to the senate. And he said, "Mr. Lincoln, before you start I would like you to remember that you are a shoemaker's son." And the whole senate laughed. They wanted to humiliate Lincoln; they could not defeat him, but they could humiliate him. But it is difficult to humiliate a man like Lincoln.

He said to the man, "I am tremendously grateful that you reminded me of my father, who is dead. I will always remember your advice. I know that I can never be such a great president as my father was a shoemaker." There was pindrop silence – the way Lincoln had taken it....

And he said to the man, "As far as I know, my father used to make shoes for your family too. If your shoes are pinching or some trouble is there – although I am not a great shoemaker I have learned the art with my father from my very childhood – I can correct it. And the same to anybody in the senate; if my father has made the shoes, and they need any correction, any improvement, I am always available – although one thing is certain, I cannot be that great. His touch was golden." And tears came to his eyes in the memory of his great father.

It does not matter: you may be a third-class president, you may be a first-class shoemaker. What fulfills is that you are enjoying what you are doing, that you are putting all your energies into it; that you don't want to be anybody else; that this is what you want to be; that you agree with nature that the part given to you to play in this drama is the right part, and you are not ready to change it even with a president or an emperor. This is real richness. This is real power.

If everybody grows to be himself, you will find the whole earth full of powerful people, of tremendous strength, intelligence, understanding, and a fulfillment, a joy that they have come home.

The sources of the talks reproduced in this volume are listed below:

CHAPTER 1 Sex: The Most Vital Energy *from*
My Way: The Way of the White Clouds, Chapter 6

CHAPTER 2 Religions Contaminate Sex Energy *from*
The First Principle, Chapter 4

CHAPTER 3 Be Rooted In Your Body... *from*
Zen: The Path of Paradox, Vol. 3,
Chapter 8, Question 5

CHAPTER 4 Brahmacharya: The Ultimate Fragrance Of Eros
from The Tantra Vision, Vol. 2, Chapter 3,
Question 4

CHAPTER 5 Key To Eternal Life *from*
The Tantra Vision, Vol. 1, Chapter 2, Question 4

CHAPTER 6 Alchemy Of Transformation *from*
The Great Pilgrimage: From Here To Here,
Chapter 25, Question 2

CHAPTER 7 Sex And Money: A Deep Association *from*
The Dhammapada: The Way of the Buddha,
Vol. 2, Chapter 4, Question 4

CHAPTER 8 I Am Not Against Money *from*
Tao: The Three Treasures,
Vol. 2, Chapter 5

CHAPTER 9 Politics: A Blind Trip Of Ego *from*
Zen: The Path of Paradox, Vol 1 Chapter 10

CHAPTER 10 Leave The Politicians Aside *from*
The New Dawn, Chapter 4

CHAPTER 11 Authenticity: Real Richness, Real Power *from*
The Transmission of the Lamp, Chapter 26

INFORMATION ABOUT
THE ORIGINAL AUDIO SERIES:

Books by Osho are transcriptions from discourses given before a live audience. All Osho discourses have been published in full as books and are also available as original audio recordings. Information about the audio recordings and the complete text archive can be found at the OSHO Library at www.osho.com.

About the Author

Osho defies categorization, reflecting everything from the individual quest for meaning to the most urgent social and political issues facing society today. His books are not written but are transcribed from recordings of extemporaneous talks given over a period of thirty-five years. Osho has been described by *The Sunday Times* in London as one of the "1000 Makers of the 20th Century" and by *Sunday Mid-Day* in India as one of the ten people – along with Gandhi, Nehru and Buddha – who have changed the destiny of India.

Osho has a stated aim of helping to create the conditions for the birth of a new kind of human being, characterized as "Zorba the Buddha" – one whose feet are firmly on the ground, yet whose hands can touch the stars. Running like a thread through all aspects of Osho's talks and meditations is a vision that encompasses both the timeless wisdom of the

East and the highest potential of Western science and technology.

He is synonymous with a revolutionary contribution to the science of inner transformation and an approach to meditation which specifically addresses the accelerated pace of contemporary life. The unique OSHO® Active Meditations™ are designed to allow the release of accumulated stress in the body and mind so that it is easier to be still and experience the thought-free state of meditation.

OSHO International Meditation Resort

Every year the OSHO® International Meditation Resort™ welcomes thousands of people from over 100 countries who come to enjoy and participate in its unique atmosphere of meditation and celebration. The 28-acre meditation resort is located about 100 miles southeast of Mumbai (Bombay), in Pune, India, in a tree-lined residential area, set against a backdrop of bamboo groves and wild jasmine, peacocks and waterfalls, The basic approach of the meditation resort is that of Zorba the Buddha: living in awareness, with a capacity to celebrate everything in life. Many visitors come to just be, to allow themselves the luxury of doing nothing. Others choose to participate in a wide variety of courses and sessions that support moving toward a more joyous and less stressful life, by combining methods of self-understanding with awareness techniques. These courses are offered through OSHO® Multiversity™ and take place in a pyramid complex next to the famous OSHO® Teerth Park.™

People can choose to practice various meditation methods, both active and passive, from a daily schedule that begins at six o'clock in the morning. Early each evening there is a meditation event that moves from dance to silent sitting, using Osho's recorded talks as an opportunity to experience inner silence without effort.

Facilities include tennis courts, a gym, sauna, Jacuzzi, a nature-shaped Olympic-sized swimming pool, classes in Zen archery, Tai chi, Chi gong, Yoga and a multitude of bodywork sessions.

The kitchen serves international gourmet vegetarian meals, made with organically grown produce. The nightlife is alive with friends dining under the stars, and with music and dancing.

Online bookings for accommodation at the OSHO˚ Guesthouse which is inside the meditation resort can be made through the website below or by sending an email to: guesthouse@osho.com

Online tours of the meditation resort, how to get there, and program information can be found at: http://www.osho.com/resort

For detailed information to participate in this meditation resort please contact:
OSHO INTERNATIONAL MEDITATION RESORT
17 Koregaon Park, Pune–411001, MS, India
Phone: +91-20-66019999 Fax:+91- 20-66019990
Email: resortinfo@osho.net Website: http://www.osho.com

 # Books by Osho in English

EARLY DISCOURSES AND WRITINGS
A Cup of Tea
Dimensions Beyond The Known
From Sex to Super-consciousness
The Great Challenge
Hidden Mysteries
I Am The Gate
The Inner Journey
Psychology of the Esoteric
Seeds of Wisdom

MEDITATION
The Voice of Silence
And Now and Here (Vol 1 & 2)
In Search of the Miraculous (Vol 1 &.2)
Meditation: The Art of Ecstasy
Meditation: The First and Last Freedom
The Path of Meditation
The Perfect Way
Yaa-Hoo! The Mystic Rose

BUDDHA AND BUDDHIST MASTERS
The Book of Wisdom
The Dhammapada: The Way of the Buddha (Vol 1-12)
The Diamond Sutra
The Discipline of Transcendence (Vol 1-4)
The Heart Sutra

INDIAN MYSTICS
Enlightenment: The Only Revolution (Ashtavakra)
Showering Without Clouds   (Sahajo)
The Last Morning Star (Daya)
The Song of Ecstasy (Adi Shankara)

BAUL MYSTICS
The Beloved (Vol 1 & 2)

KABIR
The Divine Melody
Ecstasy: The Forgotten Language
The Fish in the Sea is Not Thirsty
The Great Secret
The Guest
The Path of Love
The Revolution

JESUS AND CHRISTIAN MYSTICS
Come Follow to You (Vol 1-4)
I Say Unto You (Vol 1 & 2)
The Mustard Seed
Theologia Mystica

JEWISH MYSTICS

The Art of Dying

The True Sage

WESTERN MYSTICS

Guida Spirituale (Desiderata)

The Hidden Harmony (Heraclitus)

The Messiah (Vol 1 & 2) (Commentaries on Khalil Gibran's The Prophet)

The New Alchemy: To Turn You On (Commentaries on Mabel Collins' Light on the Path)

Philosophia Perennis (Vol 1 & 2) (The Golden Verses of Pythagoras)

Zarathustra: A God That Can Dance

Zarathustra: The Laughing Prophet (Commentaries on Nietzsche's Thus Spake Zarathustra)

SUFISM

Just Like That

Journey to the Heart

The Perfect Master (Vol 1 & 2)

The Secret

Sufis: The People of the Path (Vol 1 & 2)

Unio Mystica (Vol 1 & 2)

The Wisdom of the Sands(Vol 1 & 2)

TANTRA

Tantra: The Supreme Understanding

The Tantra Experience

The Royal Song of Saraha (same as Tantra Vision, Vol 1)

The Tantric Transformation

The Royal Song of Saraha (same as Tantra Vision, Vol 2)

The Book of Secrets: Vigyan Bhairav Tantra

THE UPANISHADS

Behind a Thousand Names (Nirvana Upanishad)

Heartbeat of the Absolute (Ishavasya Upanishad)

I Am That (Isa Upanishad)

The Message Beyond Words (Kathopanishad)

Philosophia Ultima (Mandukya Upanishad)

The Supreme Doctrine (Kenopanishad)

Finger Pointing to the Moon (Adhyatma Upanishad)

That Art Thou (Sarvasar Upanishad, Kaivalya Upanishad, Adhyatma Upanishad)

The Ultimate Alchemy, Vol 1&2 (Atma Pooja Upanishad Vol 1 &2)

Vedanta: Seven Steps to Samadhi (Akshaya Upanishad)

Flight of the Alone to the Alone (Kaivalya Upanishad)

TAO

The Empty Boat

The Secret of Secrets

Tao:The Golden Gate (Vol 1&2)

Tao:The Pathless Path (Vol 1&2)

Tao: The Three Treasures (Vol 1-4)

When the Shoe Fits

YOGA

The Path of Yoga (previously Yoga: The Alpha and the Omega (Vol 1)

Yoga: The Alpha and the Omega (Vol 2-10)

ZEN AND ZEN MASTERS

Ah, This!

Ancient Music in the Pines

And the Flowers Showered

A Bird on the Wing

Bodhidharma: The Greatest Zen Master

Communism and Zen Fire, Zen Wind

Dang Dang Doko Dang

The First Principle

God is Dead: Now Zen is the Only Living Truth

The Grass Grows By Itself

The Great Zen Master Ta Hui

Hsin Hsin Ming: The Book of Nothing

I Celebrate Myself: God is No Where, Life is Now Here

Kyozan: A True Man of Zen

Nirvana: The Last Nightmare

No Mind: The Flowers of Eternity

No Water, No Moon

One Seed Makes the Whole Earth Green

Returning to the Source

The Search: Talks on the 10 Bulls of Zen

A Sudden Clash of Thunder

The Sun Rises in the Evening

Take it Easy (Vol 1 & 2)

This Very Body the Buddha

Walking in Zen, Sitting in Zen

The White Lotus

Yakusan: Straight to the Point of Enlightenment

Zen Manifesto : Freedom From Oneself

Zen: The Mystery and the Poetry of the Beyond

Zen: The Path of Paradox (Vol 1, 2 & 3)

Zen: The Special Transmission

Zen Boxed Sets

The World of Zen (5 vol.)

Live Zen

This. This. A Thousand Times This

Zen: The Diamond Thunderbolt

Zen: The Quantum Leap from Mind to No-Mind

Zen: The Solitary Bird, Cuckoo

of the Forest

Zen: All The Colors Of The Rainbow (5 vol.)

The Buddha: The Emptiness of the Heart

The Language of Existence
The Miracle
The Original Man
Turning In

OSHO: ON THE ANCIENT MASTERS OF ZEN (7 VOLUMES)*

Dogen: The Zen Master
Hyakujo: The Everest of Zen–
With Basho's haikus
Isan: No Footprints in the Blue Sky
Joshu: The Lion's Roar
Ma Tzu: The Empty Mirror
Nansen: The Point Of Departure
Rinzai: Master of the Irrational
Each volume is also available individually.

RESPONSES TO QUESTIONS

Be Still and Know
Come, Come, Yet Again Come
The Goose is Out
The Great Pilgrimage: From Here to Here
Invitation
My Way: The Way of the White Clouds
Nowhere to Go But In
The Razor's Edge
Walk Without Feet, Fly Without Wings and
    Think Without Mind
The Wild Geese and the Water
Zen: Zest, Zip, Zap and Zing
From Bondage To Freedom
From Darkness to Light
From Death To Deathlessness

From the False to the Truth

From Unconsciousness to Consciousness

The Rajneesh Bible (Vol 2-4)

Beyond Enlightenment (Talks in Bombay)

Beyond Psychology (Talks in Uruguay)

Light on the Path (Talks in the Himalayas)

The Path of the Mystic (Talks in Uruguay)

Sermons in Stones (Talks in Bombay)

Socrates Poisoned Again After 25 Centuries (Talks in
    Greece)

The Sword and the Lotus

(Talks in the Himalayas)

The Transmission of the Lamp

(Talks in Uruguay)

OSHO'S VISION FOR THE WORLD

The Golden Future

The Hidden Splendor

The New Dawn

The Rebel

The Rebellious Spirit

THE MANTRA SERIES

Hari Om Tat Sat

Om Mani Padme Hum

Om Shantih Shantih Shantih

Sat-Chit-Anand

Satyam-Shivam-Sundram

PERSONAL GLIMPSES

Books I Have Loved

Glimpses of a Golden Childhood

Notes of a Madman

INTERVIEWS WITH THE WORLD PRESS
The Man of Truth: A Majority of One

For any information about OSHO Books, please contact:
OSHO Media International
17 Koregaon Park, Pune – 411001, MS, India
Phone: +91-20-66019999 Fax: +91-20-66019990
E-mail: distribution@osho.net
Website: http://www.osho.com

Full Circle Books by
OSHO

Meditation: The Only Way
In this fascinating collection of talks, Osho indicates how many of the difficulties facing modern humanity can be traced to a simple fact: we don't know who we are.

Freedom from the Past
Osho reveals more of his captivating vision for a new man and the new world. He shows how the current global crisis has created a sense of urgency that can help usher in a totally new way of living.

The Way of the Sufi
A parable is a way of saying things in an indirect way. Truth cannot be asserted directly. That is too violent, too aggressive, too male. Truth can only be said in a very indirect way.

The Silence of the Heart
Sufism is not an idea as such. It is a practical methodology, it is alchemy. If you understand its ways, it is going to transmute you from lower metal to higher metal.

Available at all leading bookstores.

Full Circle Books by

OSHO

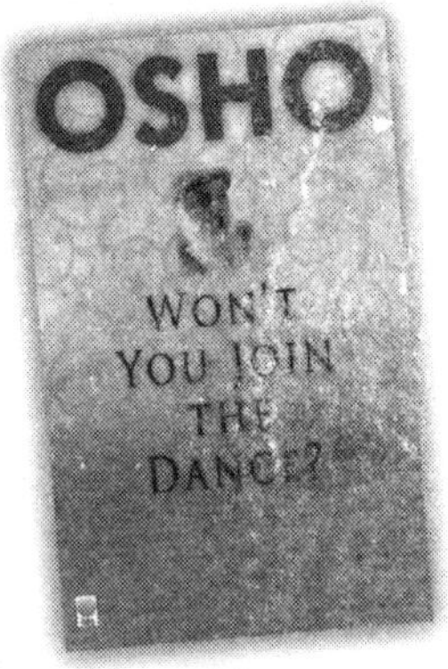
OSHO
WON'T YOU JOIN THE DANCE?

Won't You Join the Dance
That's what I teach, trust your intelligence, trust your own heart, its feelings — and even if sometimes it looks crazy to follow those feelings, go with them.

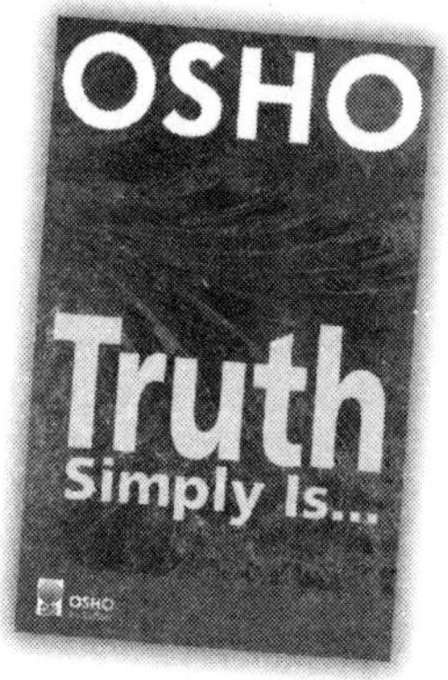
OSHO
Truth
Simply Is...

Truth Simply Is...
In this book, Osho takes us step-by-step through Sufism – How to arrive at the gentle meaning of Sufism and learn to nourish ourselves by applying it to our daily life.

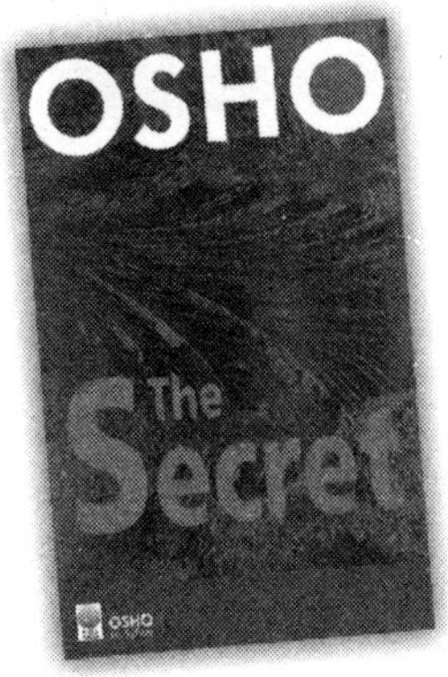
OSHO
The
Secret

The Secret
This is not really a book. It is more of a dance. And not an ordinary dance. It is Sufi Whirlwind from the heart. This book is a song, a remembrance, an embrace, a longing — *zhikr*... for that secret moment.

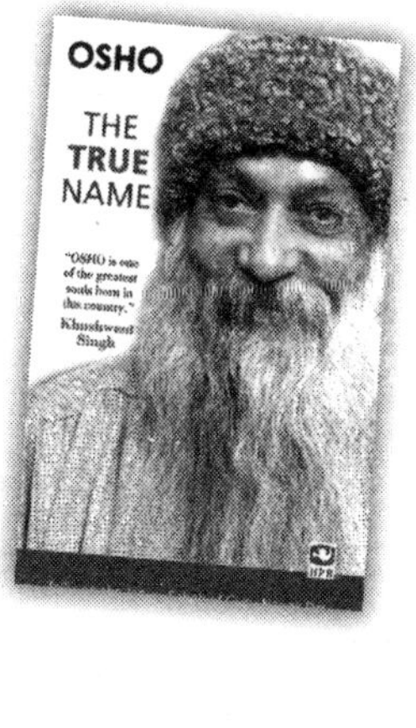
OSHO
THE
TRUE
NAME

The True Name
Talks on the Wisdom of Guru Nanak Dev
Spoken with authority, clarity, sharpness and humor, his insights address both the timeless and timely concerns that tend to escape our notice in the clamor and overload of daily life.

Available at all leading bookstores.

Full Circle Books by
OSHO

Walk without Feet, Fly without wings, Think Without Mind
This is no ordinary book – its secret lies behind your breath as you read. It's not the philosophy, no – not the wealth of information here, not even the useful tidbits that brighten your day. This is something else...

Never Born, Never Died
Rebellious and independent from childhood, Osho was born in Kuchwada, Madhya Pradesh. At twenty-one, he attained 'enlightenment'. Thereafter, he travelled throughout India giving talks and meeting people from all walks of life.

Ah This!
Osho on Zen
You are all Buddha – sleeping, dreaming, but you are Buddhas all the same. My function is not to make Buddhas out of you, because you are already that, but just to help you remember it, to remind you.

Tantra: The Supreme Understanding
Talks on the Tantric Way of Tilopa's Song of Mahamudra
Nothing much is known about Indian master Tilopa yet his mystical insight into Tantra in the form of a song passed on to his disciple Narepa, has lived on through the ages.

Available at all leading bookstores.

FULL CIRCLE

Full Circle publishes books on inspirational subjects, religion, philosophy, and natural health. The objective is to help make an attitudinal shift towards a more peaceful, loving, non-combative, non-threatening, compassionate and healing world.

We continue our commitment towards creating a peaceful and harmonious world and towards rekindling the joyous, divine nature of the human spirit.

Our fine books are available at all leading bookstores across the country and the Full Circle premium bookstores below:

Bookstores

23, Khan Market, 1st & 2nd Floor
New Delhi-110003 Tel: 011-24655641/2/3

N-16, Greater Kailash Part I Market
New Delhi-110048 Tel: 011-29245641/3/4

Number 8, Nizamuddin East Market
New Delhi-110013 Tel: 011-41826124/5

G-27, Sector-18, Noida - 201301
Tel. : 0120-4308504-07

contact@fullcirclebooks.in   www.fullcirclebooks.in

FullCircle@Chamiers, New # 106, Chamiers Road
R A Puram, Chennai-600028 Tel: 044-42030733 / 42036833
www.chamiersshop.com

Visit our online bookstore at:
www.fullcirclebooks.in

Join the
World
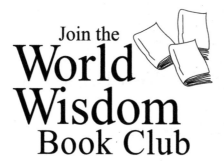
Wisdom
Book Club

GET THE BEST OF WORLD LITERATURE IN THE COMFORT OF YOUR HOME AT FABULOUS DISCOUNTS!

Benefits of the Book Club

Wherever in the world you are, you can receive the best of books at your doorstep.

- Receive FABULOUS DISCOUNTS by mail or at the **FULL CIRCLE** Bookstores in Delhi.

- Receive Exclusive Invitations to attend events being organized by **FULL CIRCLE**.

- Receive a FREE copy of the club newsletter — The World Wisdom Review — every month.

- Get UP TO 10% OFF.

Join Now!
It's simple. Just fill in the coupon overleaf and mail it to us at the address below:

FULL CIRCLE
J-40, Jorbagh Lane, New Delhi-110003
Tel: 24620063, 24621011 • Fax: 24645795
E-mail: contact@fullcirclebooks.in **www.fullcirclebooks.in**

Yes, I would like to be a member of the

World Wisdom Book Club

Name ☐ Mr ☐ Mrs ☐ Ms..

Mailing Address...

....

....

City................................... Pin.................................

Phone................................. Fax.................................

E-mail..

Profession.............................. D.O.B..........................

Areas of Interest...

....

Mail this form to:
The World Wisdom Book Club
J-40, Jorbagh Lane, New Delhi-110003
Tel: 24620063, 24621011 • Fax: 24645795
E-mail: contact@fullcirclebooks.in   *www.fullcirclebooks.in*

SEX, MONEY AND POWER